# Cooking for Your Gluten-Free Teen

Also by Carlyn Berghoff and Nancy Ross Ryan

*The Berghoff Family Cookbook*
*The Berghoff Café Cookbook*

# Cooking for Your
# GLUTEN-FREE TEEN

## Everyday Foods
## the Whole Family Will Love

by Carlyn Berghoff and Sarah Berghoff McClure

with Suzanne P. Nelson, MD, MPH, and Nancy Ross Ryan

Andrews McMeel
Publishing, LLC

Kansas City • Sydney • London

To Sarah, and to our family, for embracing our new lifestyle.

— *Carlyn*

● ● ○

To my mom and my family for tolerating my complaining for months.
To Ashley Malmquist for taking care of me when I was sick.

— *Sarah*

Andrews McMeel Publishing, LLC
an Andrews McMeel Universal company
1130 Walnut Street, Kansas City, Missouri 64106

www.andrewsmcmeel.com

13 14 15 16 17 SDB 10 9 8 7 6 5 4 3 2 1

ISBN: 978-1-4494-2760-3

Library of Congress Control Number: 2012955066

Follow Carlyn and Sarah at www.gffamilyfood.com,
on Facebook at Gluten Free Family Food,
and on Twitter @gffamilyfood and @gfreesarah.

**attention: schools and businesses**
Andrews McMeel books are available at quantity discounts with bulk purchase for educational, business, or sales promotional use. For information, please e-mail the Andrews McMeel Publishing Special Sales Department: specialsales@amuniversal.com

# contents

Foreword • by Stefano Guandalini, MD  vii

# PART I: THE NEW LIFESTYLE

Why I Wrote This Book • by Carlyn Berghoff                                3

Eating with the Enemy • by Carlyn Berghoff                               5

Nothing Helped—and Then Finally
   Something Did • by Sarah Berghoff McClure                        11

The Inside Track on Celiac • by Suzanne P. Nelson, MD, MPH              15

The Survey: Top Thirty Foods Kids Miss Most                            21

Guide to Gluten-Free Eating and Cooking • by Carlyn Berghoff           23

Eating Out: School, Restaurants,
   and Away from Home • by Sarah Berghoff McClure               29

Sharing Tips • by Suzanne P. Nelson, MD, MPH                            31

Helpful Links                                                          32

# PART II: THE COOKBOOK

The Best Place to Start                                                 36

Recipe Guidelines for Gluten-Free Cooking                              37

Lactose Intolerance, Dairy Allergies, and a Gluten-Free Diet           38

Resources for Gluten-Free Products                                      39

Chapter 1 • Breakfast and Bread                                        41

Chapter 2 • Starters and Snacks                                        73

Chapter 3 • Soups, Salads, and Sandwiches                              89

Chapter 4 • Main Dishes                                               107

Chapter 5 • Side Dishes                                               135

Chapter 6 • Desserts                                                  151

Acknowledgments  173
Metric Conversions and Equivalents  174
Index  175
About the Authors  182

# foreword

Celiac disease is an autoimmune condition affecting primarily the small intestine. If left untreated, it has serious consequences, such as osteoporosis, thyroid disease, infertility, and in some rare cases it may even lead to cancer. While the initial cause of this abnormal immune reaction in genetically susceptible individuals is not yet fully understood, once it occurs, we do know that the only way to put the disease in remission is by adhering to a strict, lifelong diet that is completely devoid of gluten, a protein found in wheat, barley, and rye.

We have very accurate screening tests and diagnostic tools to determine whether someone has celiac disease. These tests are only accurate, however, when performed *before* starting a gluten-free diet.

Non-celiac gluten sensitivity is another matter. With symptoms that are, in many cases, similar to those of celiac disease, it cannot be currently diagnosed with any laboratory test. Research is ongoing to better understand what non-celiac gluten sensitivity really is and how we can diagnose it with certainty. What we know for sure is that it is very important to test for and rule out celiac disease before coming to a diagnosis of non-celiac gluten sensitivity.

Our researchers are hard at work to find alternative therapies for celiac disease, and our ultimate goal is to find a cure that would reverse the disease in those who have it and prevent it in those who are at risk for it. We are making progress. The University of Chicago Celiac Disease Center is first in the world to develop an animal model of the disease.* This groundbreaking advance will be at the core of all future research toward a cure. With proper funding, we believe we can secure the cure in fifteen to twenty years. For more information, or to donate, please visit www.cureceliacdisease.org.

In the meantime, a strict gluten-free diet remains the only treatment. In my experience as a pediatric gastroenterologist, the transformation of my patients from, in many cases, seriously ill to full health, often within just a few short weeks of treatment, is both remarkable and rewarding. There is no question that this diet should not be taken lightly, as it can be difficult to safely navigate a world where gluten is so pervasive, but the diet is truly a miracle drug—without any of the negative consequences that often accompany a pharmaceutical regimen. And, thanks to expert and dedicated chefs such as Ms. Berghoff, it is becoming easier to make the gluten-free diet taste good, too! Enjoy her book, which is full of rich and yummy suggestions!

Stefano Guandalini, MD
*Professor and Chief*
*Section of Pediatric Gastroenterology*
*University of Chicago*
*Founder and Medical Director, Celiac Disease Center*

THE UNIVERSITY OF CHICAGO
CELIAC
DISEASE CENTER

FROM CARE TO CURE

*In medical research, animal models have a disease, either existing or induced, that is similar to a human disease. This allows for research into the disease without using a human patient.

# PART I

# The New Lifestyle

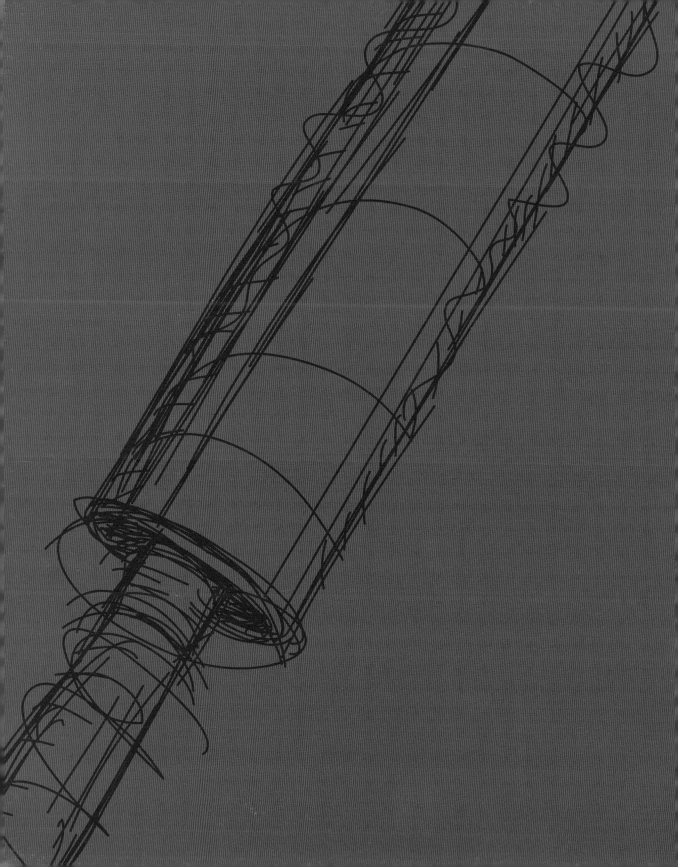

# WHY I WROTE THIS BOOK
by Carlyn Berghoff

Every author has to answer the basic question: Why write this book? My answer: Because I'm not only the chef at one of Chicago's most famous, historic restaurants, which serves all kinds of wheat-based foods, but also the mom of a teenager who was diagnosed with celiac disease.

The 2010 U.S. Census reports there are 30 million American teens, ages thirteen to nineteen. According to one study, one in every 133 Americans is affected by celiac disease.[1] (Those statistics do not include the number of individuals who have non-celiac gluten sensitivity.) There are no statistics for the number of teens affected; however, every

one of those Americans affected by celiac disease will be, is, or was a teen. Teens are the bridge from childhood to adulthood. Teens are our future. Teens are our legacy.

The only sure and effective treatment for celiac disease is a gluten-free diet, and teens present special challenges to that treatment.

If you are a parent of a young child with celiac disease, you are the person responsible for providing, maintaining, and monitoring their food. Not so with teenagers. They are semi-autonomous. They eat away from home; they fix food for themselves at home; they make choices. And many of the food choices they make are more adventurous than the choices they made when they were a few years younger. Teens go to restaurants: Asian, Mexican, Italian, regional American.

Their palate broadens and they develop a taste for stir-fry and tacos and linguine Alfredo as well as barbecue. Cooking for teenagers is a challenge and it is fun!

Teenagers lead busy lives, and they are peer-sensitive. They don't want to appear different, and they want to eat what their friends and everybody else eats.

How well they learn the celiac diet—what they can and cannot eat—and how well they train themselves to stick with it form the habits that will last them a lifetime. And, to a very large extent, these habits determine their well-being.

It is my hope that this book will help them and their families by using the guidelines to gluten-free shopping, cooking, and eating, and especially by cooking the recipes. The recipes include teenage favorite

1. Fasano et al., A multi-center study on the seroprevalence of celiac disease in the United States among both at risk and not at risk groups. *Archives of Internal Medicine*. February 2003.

foods and dishes the whole family will love. They are easy to prepare and not nearly as expensive as buying prepared prepackaged or frozen gluten-free foods. And, when Sarah's (and Lindsey's and Todd's) friends help themselves to seconds of the gluten-free dishes at our house, we know the food is good. As the old adage states: "The proof of the pudding is in the eating."

Cheers!

Carlyn Berghoff

# EATING WITH THE ENEMY

by Carlyn Berghoff

My family has been a restaurant family for more than one hundred years. I practically grew up at our Chicago-landmark German restaurant, the Berghoff, eating and cooking plenty of schnitzel, rye bread, creamed spinach, spaetzle, noodles, apple pancakes, and Black Forest cake, which meant wheat and its gluten in every imaginable form.

When I attended chef's school at the Culinary Institute of America, the term "gluten free" was not even part of our vocabulary. Bread and wheat flour played a huge role in the cooking curriculum. After that, I opened my own catering business, and my menu was rich with bread, breading, crumbs, sauces, gravy, and desserts, a gold mine of gluten.

Along the way, I married Jim McClure and we had three great kids: Lindsey, Sarah,

and Todd. Cooking was just as central to my home life as it was to my professional life. We have always eaten family dinner together. Just look up "dinner table proverbs" on the Internet, and you will be awash in pithy sayings from all cultures about the importance of dining together. My favorite is an Italian proverb *"Chi mangia bene, vive bene,"* or "Who eats well, lives well." How was I to know that we were neither eating well nor living well? I didn't have a clue that my freshly cooked, nutritionally balanced, delicious meals were going to make one of my children deathly ill.

## The First Kitchen Revolution

As a mother and a cook, I have always kept informed on nutritional information. One year

before Sarah, my then-twelve-year-old daughter, got sick, I inventoried every edible morsel in my pantry, fridge, and freezer in a campaign to get rid of all processed, over-refined foods. The push came from my good friend Dena Mendes, a passionate advocate of eating and cooking unprocessed, whole, natural foods. She was also ahead of me in cooking and writing about gluten- and dairy-free foods on her Dena's Healthy U website. Although Dena wanted me to go the whole nine yards to a gluten-free pantry because she had this "thing" about gluten, I told her: "One step at a time. First let me get rid of all the processed foods, sugars, and empty calories; switch to whole grains; and then we'll talk about the next step." Coincidentally, this cleanup ironically removed a large percent of gluten in

5

the form of crackers, chips, pretzels, and other savory and sweet snacks, and white flour. My pantry was definitely nutritionally improved by switching to whole grains and organic fruits and vegetables; however, it was not gluten free, and I didn't even entertain the concept of making it so.

In August of 2009, Sarah, who had just started junior high school, began to have random stomachaches. I diagnosed her symptoms as pre–junior high jitters. By late September, at her first doctor's visit with her pediatrician, Sarah was complaining about nausea, sore throat, and numerous aches and pains throughout her body—and her first bout of diarrhea. "Maybe I have strep throat," she said.

When I visited the doctor with her, I learned that my already slight, petite daughter had lost five pounds since her previous physical in April. The loss of five pounds in five months was scary. The doctor took a throat culture; it came back negative. The diagnosis was not strep but a virus. She advised there was no medication for it, and time would take care of it. Sarah's symptoms decreased, but from that moment on, she never felt really well.

## Trick or Treat

When Halloween came (the one holiday where all my kids get to eat any kind of candy they want), Sarah didn't want to go out trick-or-treating with friends. She had a stomachache and diarrhea, and for the first time, I noticed she had deep, dark circles under her eyes and her skin looked pale and gray. "Oh," I thought, "It's winter and she hasn't been out in the sun."

After Halloween, we visited the doctor once more, and Sarah had lost another five pounds! We still didn't know what, if anything, was wrong.

## Mother of the Year Award

The Friday after Thanksgiving is known in my corner of the restaurant world as Black Friday. It's the busiest, craziest day of the year. Kids are off school; moms and dads frequently take off work; they all go shopping for the good sales. Then they come to the restaurant for lunch and dinner. So I asked my girls to come to the restaurant to help out, as they do every year. Sarah said she was too sick to come: stomachache and diarrhea.

"Really?!" I said. "Or are you just trying to get out of work?"

When I look back on Thanksgiving and what she ate, it is now painfully clear: stuffing and gravy, rolls, pumpkin pie and German chocolate cake: gluten and more gluten.

But I tended to tune out her complaints because, of all my children, Sarah has always been more sensitive to how she is feeling, and her physical symptoms and complaints followed no pattern. They were (or seemed) completely random. She didn't come to the restaurant to help on Friday, but when Saturday came around, so did she, and she seemed fine.

I went into holiday work mode. Everyone in the restaurant business and catering business knows what a busy and crucial time of year it is between Thanksgiving and New Year's. In January, we took a family vacation to Florida. The very first night there, Sarah woke me up and said, "I think I'm dying." She was suffering from a horrific stomachache. "It never seems to go away," she moaned.

"How long have you been feeling this way?" I asked her.

"All month," she replied.

"Yes," I thought to myself, "I'm gonna win that Mother of the Year Award. For sure!"

Our pediatrician was on vacation and I knew it would

do me no good to call whoever was on call because they didn't have Sarah's charts and would not have the chance to examine her. And if we went to the ER in Florida, she would get poked and prodded, it would take hours, and we might not get a definitive diagnosis.

So we called "Dr. Bonnie" (Dr. Bonnie Typlin), a family friend and MD who had known Sarah all her life. Sarah talked to her, described her symptoms: stomachache, diarrhea, felt like throwing up, and a burning feeling in the middle of her chest.

Dr. Bonnie heard symptoms of acid reflux and said that we should go on the Internet and check out the foods that could cause it. She warned us that they would be different than we might expect, and they were. She recommended an over-the-counter antacid before and after meals and suggested that Sarah keep a food journal to see if specific foods caused symptoms.

## Happy Birthday

The first food entered in Sarah's journal was chocolate cake, and the first symptom was agony. Sarah ate one piece of Todd's homemade birthday cake and spent the entire night howling in pain. The cake had flour, butter, eggs, sugar, and chocolate. We had no clue which ingredient or ingredients caused the violent reaction. After that episode, she felt better, drank a lot of tea, and didn't eat much. She had very low energy, and her coloring was not getting better despite the fact that we were in Florida, the Sunshine State. When I took a good, hard look at her, I saw that Sarah was skin and bones, so thin, I had to buy her new clothes. In retrospect, I realize she was completely malnourished.

## Mystery Solved

When we returned home from the trip, Sarah saw her regular pediatrician. We told the pediatrician what Dr. Bonnie had said, and the pediatrician said she would start Sarah on an acid reflux drug that would take two weeks to take effect.

"We can't wait two weeks," I said.

"Let's do some tests, then," the doctor said.

"Tests for what?" I asked the doctor out of Sarah's earshot.

"Celiac, cancer, and Crohn's disease," she replied.

"Which should I pray for?" I asked.

"Celiac. Definitely celiac," she replied.

"What's celiac?" I asked.

"Complete intolerance to gluten," she replied.

And that was the first I had ever heard of celiac disease or a life-threatening reaction to gluten.

Within twenty-four hours, the doctor called. "Sarah has celiac disease," she said, and she recommended we see Dr. Suzanne Nelson, a pediatric gastroenterologist. Dr. Nelson specializes in children's gastro-enterology, or diseases of the digestive track from one end to the other. While Sarah's blood tests had indicated celiac disease, we needed to do biopsies of the throat, stomach, and small intestine to make sure there was no damage and, as I later learned, to rule out other, worse diseases. She told Sarah *not* to stop eating foods with gluten because celiac shows up in the small intestine, and in the absence of gluten, the body starts to heal itself. The gold standard test for celiac is a simple biopsy of the small intestine. If someone has celiac disease, the villi (little finger-like projections that absorb nutrients from food in the intestines) are flattened and impaired. That explains why Sarah lost weight: She was not absorbing nutrients from what she ate; she was truly starving. The best way to understand Sarah's condition is to imagine her stomach lined with plastic wrap. Nothing—no vitamins, minerals, calories—gets absorbed. She eats, drinks, and eliminates, but all the nutrients simply pass through.

After the biopsy, Dr. Nelson diagnosed celiac but no other diseases. Sarah and I made an appointment to meet with Dr. Nelson's staff nutritionist, Betsy Hjelmgren. "We'll talk about the journey ahead—what it will take to get gluten out of Sarah's system, how she must change eating habits, what medicines she might need and for how long," she reassured us.

## A Steep Learning Curve

By the time we met with Betsy, it was almost Sarah's thirteenth birthday. She had been sick for almost a year. Betsy did a great job of explaining what we needed to do in our kitchen to keep Sarah safe. I thought I could easily translate her instructions into action because I ran my restaurant/catering kitchen with systems and checklists. I was not prepared, however, for how steep the learning curve of this new system would be. I also realized that for the average cook this transition would be overwhelming, and for someone who doesn't cook, it would seem almost impossible. For that reason, I have created a kitchen guide to cooking gluten free (see page 23).

For the newly diagnosed celiac sufferer to get better, it helps to stop eating out altogether at first and to stop buying prepackaged foods. In time, the celiac patient learns what, how, and where to eat out (see "Eating Out: School, Restaurants, and Away from Home," page 29), and the cook learns which fresh, prepared, and prepackaged foods are gluten free (see "Grocery Shopping," page 26). The first step is to remove all gluten from the diet and kitchen at home. Teens and kids have the added step of learning how to eat gluten free at school.

After her diagnosis, Sarah was relieved to know she was not dying, but she was dazed by all the information coming at her. Nutritionist Betsy gave Sarah food lists, a diet plan, leaflets, pamphlets, and the names of support groups and Internet resources. It took Sarah six months to absorb it all, translate it mentally, adjust emotionally, and make the new lifestyle her own.

One of the most difficult adjustments was to eating food prepared from the gluten-free mixes available on the market. Chocolate cake was a good example. The day of Sarah's thirteenth birthday, I baked her a chocolate cake from a gluten-free mix. The finished cake was "sandy" and gummy in texture and tasted terrible. Sarah took one bite and looked at me, the chef, and said "*Really*, Mom?" And, because we hadn't yet realized she was also intolerant to chocolate and lactose, it made her sick. Happy birthday, Sarah.

## Gluten Free for One or All?

The first question I asked myself was, "Which would work better for our family: to have everyone eat a gluten-free diet, or just Sarah?" I carefully considered the pros and cons of each plan. If Sarah was the only family member on a gluten-free diet, the kitchen, ingredients, equipment, and refrigerator and freezer would have to be divided and separated so her food would not be cross-contaminated with gluten. It also meant I would be cooking two different menus every time we ate together as a family. It meant that every time Sarah or I opened the refrigerator, we would wonder whether the other kids had helped themselves to the peanut butter and repeatedly dipped in a knife that they were using to spread the peanut butter on a slice of wheat bread. After being so very sick, Sarah was afraid to eat anything. I opted for an entirely gluten-free family.

## The Second Kitchen Revolution

When I put the gluten-free kitchen and menu into action, my other kids, both teens, revolted. Lindsey and Todd were upset, and their battle cry was, "What?! No bread, no cake, no cookies, no pizza?" Notice they didn't bemoan the loss of lettuce, carrots, or broccoli. I promised we would find a store-bought or homemade substitute for everything they missed most. I told them they were welcome to eat whatever they wanted at school, at friends' houses, and at restaurants. However, they could not bring food home with them or store it in the pantry or refrigerator. I promised we could order pizza delivery—regular for them and gluten free for Sarah—because the regular pizza would be prepared outside the home and the delivery box could be kept separate and any leftovers disposed of. And I stressed that

this was what we needed to do to keep Sarah safe. After a really short time, and after eating my homemade gluten-free bread, cookies, pizza, and cake, they stopped complaining and started bombarding me with requests: "How about ribs? Can you make your chicken noodle soup this way? What about pancakes?" And, what they considered the most far-out request of all: "Doughnuts?" I'm happy to say I managed to do it all (and the proof is in this book).

## A Clean Sweep

After Sarah's confirmation test with Dr. Nelson and the meeting with nutritionist Betsy Hjelmgren, I spent an entire weekend cleaning the kitchen and bathroom, made extensive lists, and got rid of everything with gluten. Vitamins, cosmetics, some shampoos, and even toothpastes can contain gluten. The Celiac Disease Foundation website (www.celiac.org) became my best source of information about gluten in nearly everything, especially cosmetics, the medicine cabinet, and vitamins and supplements. We went to many grocery stores to replace foods and snacks with gluten-free alternatives, and to drug and specialty stores to replace cosmetics and vitamins.

## The School Lunch

Next we dealt with lunch at school. How was Sarah to eat in the cafeteria? She wasn't. So what were we to pack for lunch, and how and where was she to eat? It took a call to the school's cafeteria and school nurse to work out a system for Sarah to use the microwave oven in the nurse's office to reheat food she had packed, because the microwaves in the school cafeteria were gluten contaminated from English muffins, bagels, muffins, hot dogs in buns, and hamburgers in buns—all familiar school foods.

## Cooking Gluten Free

At home, I began to cook gluten free. In addition to developing recipes that were appealing to my family, three members of which were teenagers, I tried every prepared packaged snack, mix, and frozen and refrigerated gluten-free "convenience" food I could lay my hands on. Many, perhaps most, were a huge disappointment because they lacked flavor or had dreadful texture. Some were hugely expensive (for example, 3 pounds of gluten-free flour for $19, and one brownie mix for $19). I researched online, read labels in stores, and consulted dozens of gluten-free cookbooks. Most cookbooks were disappointing as well. Many recipes were difficult to prepare, and the selection did not appeal to my teenagers.

It became my number one priority to create some normalcy in the house when it came to eating. I learned that breakfast was by far the easiest meal. Lunch was harder because packing only foods that could be eaten at room temperature became monotonous, and we needed to find foods that could be reheated in the microwave at the nurse's office at school. Dinner was not so bad once I found convenience foods everyone liked and developed recipes to replace my family's former favorites (pizza, pasta, lasagna, cake, cookies, and all the usual suspects).

## The Good News

By Sarah's fourteenth birthday, she had gained back the ten pounds she had lost; she has grown taller, her color is good, she looks healthy, is active in her chosen sport (crew), and is on the road to complete recovery.

For me, going gluten free was overwhelming, as it can be for anyone. In the beginning, some products seemed exorbitantly expensive, grocery shopping was daunting, and cooking methods seemed unfamiliar. You will, as I did, stand in the grocery aisles, pulling out your hair and wondering, "Which one shall I try?" You will make a selection, go home, prepare it, and your family will turn their collective noses up at it. And it will have been expensive. The transition is a journey that doesn't happen overnight. It is, however, a journey you must take.

Our journey led us to write this book and share everything we learned. In the pages that follow, you will read how to set up your kitchen, what foods are naturally gluten free, which foods and ingredients have hidden gluten, and which prepared convenience foods and mixes we have had great success with (see "Don't Reinvent the Wheel," page 22). First and foremost, the recipes taste great, and the ingredients are easy to find, especially now that new gluten-free products come on the market every day. The cooking methods will become automatic and natural, and you will find that the new gluten-free lifestyle will benefit every member of your family. If you are at the beginning of creating a gluten-free kitchen (or dedicated gluten-free areas in the kitchen) and cooking gluten free, my hope is that Sarah and I have done a lot of the hardest work for you, to make your journey less difficult and more enjoyable.

# NOTHING HELPED— AND THEN FINALLY SOMETHING DID

by Sarah Berghoff McClure

If I had to say what it was like before I found out I had celiac disease, I would have to say I was sick all the time. I kept losing weight until I went down to seventy pounds. I had headaches all the time, and sometimes a fever. I was on the verge of throwing up 24/7. I had constant diarrhea. I had heartburn and acid reflux every day, and I remember thinking, "What is wrong with me? This is getting annoying." They gave me pills for acid reflux, but nothing helped. We saw my pediatrician a lot.

I was in seventh grade, and I took it seriously. I was working hard to keep my grades up, and I ran track. My life consisted of food, homework, school, and track. I didn't have time to be sick. I would hang out with friends, but I never did sleepovers at their houses. I was afraid I was going to get sick.

**A Bad Holiday Season**

After Thanksgiving, the year I was twelve, I got really sick, but I still didn't have a clue why. My hair started falling out, and when I looked in the mirror, I saw huge black-and-blue circles around my eyes. I looked like a ghost! I ate the usual stuff for Thanksgiving dinner—stuffing, gravy, and pie—and got really sick afterwards. Still no clue.

On Halloween, I went trick-or-treating to two houses, then I felt sick and came home. I thought, "Oh, no, I'm going to be up all night with a stomach-ache." But in the morning, I woke up okay, and I was fine at school because I was with my friends and distracted. But then came dinner, and there was no escape. Whatever I ate made me sick all over again.

By the Christmas holidays, I was so sick, I thought I was dying. I thought I had cancer. I don't remember how that entered my brain, maybe because my brother's godfather had non-Hodgkin's lymphoma. I remember saying, "I think I'm dying." I meant it. Nothing can more scare the crap out of you than the thought of dying.

We called Dr. Bonnie, an old family friend, and she suggested I go on an acid reflux diet. No tomatoes, no peppermints, no foods that cause acidity. She said keep a food log. I did it very well at first, but nothing changed. I didn't feel any better, so I stopped keeping track. My brother Todd's birthday was December 29, and we had chocolate birthday cake. I had one piece, and, oh, was I sick.

When we got back to Chicago and saw our doctor, she did tons of blood work. Turns out, I was lucky. Well, I was lucky that I wasn't dying. The tests came back as positive for celiac disease and I also had a case of low-grade anemia. The doctor said that because the test came out positive for celiac disease, I would have to go see another doctor. But, of course, she left out the tiny detail of having a tube stuck down my throat. Oh, what a joy.

### Seeing Dr. Nelson

When I first saw Dr. Nelson, she surprised me by telling me to eat as much gluten as I could before she did the biopsy test. She said, "Shove the wheat!" and that's what I did for a whole week. And guess what, not one stomachache. And that's another thing about celiac disease. The symptoms come and go when you least expect them. Sometimes I think I will be sick and I'm not, and sometimes I'm really sick and don't see it coming. But that's why you have to get the test, because it's

the only way to really tell for sure. Dr. Nelson told me that celiac symptoms were strange because they fit so many different diseases.

## My Thirteenth Birthday

By the time my birthday came, I had already seen the nutritionist, Betsy Hjelmgren. I was already on the gluten-free diet and I already knew what I could and couldn't eat. And it wasn't easy. I remember I wanted a bagel at Panera and I couldn't have it. So I had a couple of fits here and there. One was at Subway. I loved Subway. The Subway tuna sandwich is my complete favorite. I also remember going to a restaurant that had this really cool drink, but they weren't sure if it was gluten free, so I couldn't have it. I get really angry with waiters when they don't know what's in their food. I think to myself, "Well, you can't *think* it doesn't have gluten, you have to *know* it doesn't, or else you will be stuck with a throwing-up thirteen-year-old."

For my thirteenth birthday, my mom baked a gluten-free chocolate cake from a mix. I was looking forward to having chocolate cake again. It was horrible, and I still got so sick.

Later on, I learned I am also intolerant to chocolate.

## Gluten Free Isn't Easy, but It's Doable

After awhile, I started learning how to deal with the problems of being gluten free. The first problem was lunch. I could never eat cafeteria food at school, so I had to pack my lunch at home. I didn't really feel bad about having to pack it, but I did get annoyed because I had to carry it. At first, I used the microwave in the nurse's office to heat my lunch. Then I discovered that if I brought my stuff in containers and heated it only in the containers, never out, then I could use the microwave in the lunchroom.

I also learned that, for lunch, it's easier to make a sandwich or reheat leftovers. At first, I packed a lot of peanut butter sandwiches, but I got so sick of them that I now hate peanut butter sandwiches. So I made a list of favorites for lunch. My number one favorite is a turkey sandwich with gluten-free mayo. When it comes to leftovers, my favorite is lasagna.

Breakfast is really the most important meal, and I have some gluten-free banana bread, maybe an egg, some gluten-free

cereal—or one of my mom's disgusting smoothies. For snacks, I can eat crackers or corn chips, all gluten free, or maybe some fruit.

Dinner at home is whatever Mom makes. My favorite is ribs. But forget fruit for dessert. It's overrated. The baker at the Berghoff restaurant is named Chon, and he makes a wonderful gluten-free spice cake with frosting.

When I go to friends' houses for a birthday party or to hang out, I normally have to bring my own food. When people ask me what's wrong, I'm too lazy to go into the whole thing, so I usually just say, "I'm allergic to gluten," and drop it. But I have told a couple of friends the whole story. And if a friend of the family asks and it's legit—they're really interested—then I take time to explain.

## Life Goes On

After I started the diet, I really stuck to it. People ask me am I ever tempted to eat something with gluten. No! It's not worth getting sick again. It took me about a year to completely detox from gluten, but I felt better the minute I stopped eating it. I gained back the weight I lost, and when I look in the mirror, I see my familiar face.

At first, after the diagnosis, I worried a lot about my health. I freaked every time I got a stomachache and I drove my mom crazy. But it's gotten so much better. And once I really knew what was wrong, I could talk to people about it: my mom, the doctor. And I'm really lucky after all because it's only celiac, not something worse. Best of all, with the way I eat now compared with the way I used to eat and how most of my friends eat, I'll be healthier than anyone I know!

# THE INSIDE TRACK ON CELIAC

by Suzanne P. Nelson, MD, MPH

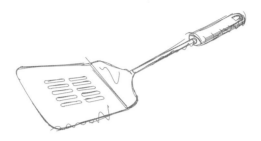

As a pediatric gastroenterologist—that is, a doctor who takes care of children with digestive problems—it is never easy to tell kids like Sarah the news: "You have a disease."

And while I am never happy to tell patients, "You have celiac disease," part of me is always relieved, because I know the child is going to be okay. Celiac disease is one of the few diseases I treat that don't require any medication (and, therefore, pose no risk of drug side effects) and that can be managed entirely by diet. Although, at the moment, doctors cannot cure celiac disease, we do know that a strict, gluten-free diet puts the disease in remission, and many people have no symptoms at all.

Does this mean that celiac disease is a minor condition, something to be taken lightly?

Absolutely not. As I explained to Sarah and Carlyn, if left untreated, the disease can increase the chances for developing weak bones (osteoporosis, which can cause fractures), small bowel cancer, infertility, and other autoimmune conditions such as insulin-dependent diabetes and thyroid disease. Untreated celiac disease can also adversely affect a child's mood, development, and growth. That's why early diagnosis and treatment are so important and can dramatically improve a child's life.

If you have celiac disease, you are not alone. Estimates suggest that about 1 percent of Americans have the disease. Current research further suggests that celiac disease is becoming increasingly common. Many people have the disease and don't even know it.

## What Is Celiac Disease?

Celiac disease is an immune system–mediated digestive disease that causes inflammation or irritation of the small intestine when gluten is ingested. To develop celiac disease, one must carry certain genes—but most people who carry these genes never develop the disease. This explains why, despite the fact that celiac disease is genetically based, Sarah was the only person in her immediate family to suffer from it. Although the exact causal details are unknown, something triggers genetically susceptible people to develop the condition. Once these people start eating gluten, they may develop celiac disease at any age. And once they have the disease, they will be unable to tolerate (or eat) gluten in any form for the rest of their lives.

Celiac disease is not a type of food allergy. Although both may result in dietary restrictions, the underlying cause is different. Moreover, children with celiac disease will not stop breathing or develop hives—common allergic reactions—if exposed to gluten.

Although today one reads and hears much about celiac disease in the popular media, it is hardly a new disease. Remarkably, Aretaeus of Cappadocia wrote about this condition in the second century A.D. Samuel Gee, an English physician, published the first modern clinical description of celiac disease in 1888, observing, "If the patient can be cured at all, it must be by means of diet."[1]

## What Is Gluten?

Gluten is a protein found in all varieties of wheat (including spelt, triticale, and Kamut), barley, and rye. Some sources of gluten are obvious: breads, baked goods, gravies, puddings, soups, sauces, and so forth. But there are hundreds of hidden sources of gluten, such as some brands of ice cream, soy sauce, and deli meats, and even some medicines and vitamins (see

1. Samuel J. Gee, *St. Bartholomew's Hospital Reports,* 24 (1888):17.

"Hidden Sources of Gluten," page 27).

Gluten causes inflammation in the small intestine, where nutrients from the food we eat are absorbed. The inflammation can damage the villi, which line the small intestine and look like tiny fingers sticking up. Inflammation flattens the villi and can interfere with nutrient absorption.

## What Are the Symptoms of Celiac Disease?

There are many possible symptoms of celiac disease (see "Possible Signs and Symptoms of Celiac Disease," page 17)—yet none of these symptoms occurs only with celiac disease. Thus, primary care providers such as your pediatrician can easily overlook the condition. Sometimes a physician may not request a test for celiac disease because the child is still growing. Indeed, many of the children I have diagnosed with the disease have shown good growth. Because the symptoms of celiac disease often develop gradually, parents may not bring their child to be evaluated, or a physician may initially monitor the child's symptoms and try to reassure the parents that "nothing is wrong." Consequently,

many parents of children with celiac disease tell me they feel bad because their child was sick for so long before being diagnosed. A delay in diagnosis is, however, typical. Hindsight is always 20/20.

Sarah was twelve when I diagnosed her with celiac disease. Although bright and pretty, she was short for her age and suffered severe stomachaches. The stomachaches were initially intermittent and then became constant. By the time I first saw Sarah, she had lost several pounds during the previous few months. Sarah showed only a few of the hundreds of possible signs and symptoms that celiac disease can exhibit (see "Possible Signs and Symptoms of Celiac Disease," page 17). These include constipation, diarrhea, stomachaches, bloating, gas, indigestion, decreased or increased appetite, irritability, nausea and vomiting, and unexplained weight loss. Lactose intolerance can also be present, usually resolving after a gluten-free diet is begun.

The bottom line? One can suffer from celiac disease with major or minor symptoms—or with no symptoms at all. Children at risk to develop celiac disease should therefore be screened, even if they don't have symptoms at the time.

These children include first-degree relatives of patients with celiac disease, and children with type 1 diabetes or autoimmune thyroiditis, Down syndrome, Turner syndrome, Williams syndrome, IgA deficiency, and dermatitis herpetiformis.

• • •

## Possible Signs and Symptoms of Celiac Disease

Abdominal pain
Anemia (from iron deficiency)
Anorexia (decreased appetite)
Anxiety
Arthritis
Bloating
Bone loss (osteopenia/ osteoporosis)
Constipation
Delayed puberty
Dental enamel defects
Depression

Diarrhea
Distended abdomen
Epilepsy (with occipital calcification)
Fatigue
Foul-smelling stool
Gassiness
Growth failure
Hair loss
Infertility
Irritability
Joint pain

Lactose intolerance
Liver and biliary tract disorders
Malnutrition
Miscarriage
Mouth sores
Rash called dermatitis herpetiformis
Short stature
Tingling of hands or feet
Vitamin or mineral deficiencies
Vomiting
Weight loss

• • •

## Diagnosis: Get the Biopsy!

If I suspect celiac disease, as Sarah's pediatrician did, I will order a blood test for specific antibodies. Although no test is perfect, and all tests can yield "false positive" and "false negative" results, this test is very accurate, and it represents the first step.

If the patient tests positive for these antibodies, as Sarah did, then I discuss the "gold standard" test for celiac disease: a biopsy of the small bowel.

This involves a procedure called an upper endoscopy. While the patient is sedated, or under anesthesia, I pass a thin flexible tube called an endoscope through the mouth and advance it into the esophagus, stomach, and the first part of the small intestine, called the duodenum. Multiple biopsies need to be taken of the small intestine, because celiac can be a spotty condition, seen in one area but not another. These biopsies are then processed, and viewed under a microscope, to see if

the condition of the tissue typifies the damage done by celiac disease. It is very important that the child is eating gluten regularly before the test to prevent false normal results.

I am often asked if this expensive and invasive biopsy is really necessary. Can't the child simply start a gluten-free diet, to see if her symptoms disappear? I try to reassure families that in the hands of an experienced gastroenterologist, the biopsy is safe, causes minimal (if any) pain, and provides valuable information. Since we are considering a lifelong dietary change for the child, we should want to know for sure that the correct diagnosis has been made. The antibody test for celiac disease is not always right. Changing to a gluten-free diet can be a big adjustment for children and families, not to mention quite costly. Therefore, I believe it is wise to know for sure—and that requires a biopsy.

Many of the patients whom I have treated over the years who failed to have the biopsy have regretted their decision. Somewhere down the line, they wonder, "Do I really have celiac disease?" With a positive biopsy finding in hand, patients are more likely to adhere to the gluten-free diet.

It is also important to note that not everyone who feels better on a gluten-free diet has celiac disease. Some individuals may just be "gluten sensitive." For example, autistic children, or those suffering with irritable bowel, may benefit from a gluten-restricted diet; these children do not, however, have celiac disease. Biopsies of the small intestine only diagnose people with celiac disease, not with gluten sensitivity.

So why is it important to know what condition your child may have, if gluten restriction may improve all these conditions? Because if one has celiac disease, one needs to be totally gluten free: It is unsafe to eat any gluten.

## Treatment: Simple and Effective

Treatment of celiac disease is simple and effective: a gluten-free diet. That's it.

Once Sarah's biopsies came back positive for celiac disease, Sarah and Carlyn met with my nutritionist, Betsy Hjelmgren, to learn about the gluten-free diet. During this session, they learned not only what Sarah needed to avoid, but also the many foods she could still eat. They learned about sources of gluten contamination and how to ensure Sarah was still going to obtain all the important vitamins and nutrients on a restricted diet. Finally, they were given everything that had been discussed in writing along with a list of resources, so they could refer to it as they adapted to a new diet and a new lifestyle.

Sometimes parents tell me they feel bad for "depriving" their child of gluten. Yet we know that all children, at one time or another, are "deprived" of something they want—maybe a certain toy, a video game, car, swimming pool, having two married parents, a particular boyfriend or girlfriend, or admission to the "perfect" college. That's life, however. As parents, we need to model and discuss with our children how to focus on what they can have and how to make the best of it. Yes, it's a challenge, but one can turn their dietary restriction into an important life lesson. They are not losing gluten; they're gaining well-being.

## Eating Well Gluten Free

What can you eat on a gluten-free diet? Plenty. Fresh fruits, vegetables, meats, poultry, and seafood are all allowed, as long as they are not prepared with something that contains gluten. Safe foods also include beans, corn, eggs, potatoes, and rice.

This book will help you make many delicious gluten-free recipes. There are also many gluten-free products on the market, and their availability is increasing over time, as more and more people without celiac disease choose to follow a gluten-free diet.

Children with celiac disease do need to take a multivitamin every day. This is particularly important after initial diagnosis, to replace nutrients lost due to malabsorption caused by the gluten damage. It is also important to provide B vitamins, since many gluten-free grain products are not fortified with B vitamins like the standard wheat-based products. Most multivitamins are gluten free, but not all, so read the label carefully!

After transitioning to a gluten-free diet, some children notice a change in their bowel movements. Constipation can occur if white rice is replacing wheat flour, or diarrhea can occur if fiber-rich grains are added in large amounts too quickly. Some children might lose weight as they adjust to a new diet, and others may gain too much weight because many processed gluten-free foods are higher in fat than their gluten-containing counterparts. Moreover, the GI tract may absorb nutrients better once it heals from the gluten damage. Being aware of these possible concerns will allow you to adjust your child's diet according to his or her needs.

Families often tell me they feel overwhelmed at first with all the new information and the prospect of changing to a gluten-free diet. As with many things in life, however, the hardest part is often the first step. Once one starts the needed changes, the path becomes much easier—and

eventually becomes routine. It constantly amazes me how well most families adapt to this big change. I also love seeing and hearing about how children with celiac disease take charge of the situation, and teach their relatives and neighbors about living gluten free.

## Gluten Free 100 Percent

I told Sarah and her mother, as I tell all my families, to aim at being totally gluten free. Why? Because even a small amount of gluten can damage the small intestine. Studies show that someone with celiac disease can react to as little as $\frac{1}{8}$ to $\frac{1}{64}$ teaspoon of wheat flour. Damage to the small intestine can happen even if one doesn't exhibit any obvious symptoms. But one should also realize that no one is perfect: Occasionally, gluten will sneak into the diet. So, aim for 100 percent gluten free, but also accept the fact that there will be slipups, and don't beat yourself up about them. As long as the slipups are rare, they will not affect the overall long-term health of a child with celiac disease.

In my experience, teenagers comply the most poorly, particularly those with less severe symptoms. I tell parents

bluntly that kids will cheat, especially teenagers. It's important, therefore, to create an environment where kids can tell their parents openly if they have cheated.

Parents need to set a good example. Don't allow gluten on some "special occasion" because you may feel bad for your child. Besides being unhealthy for your child, this practice sends the message that it is okay not to comply with the diet if you don't feel like it that day. Encourage your child to be the expert and to educate those around them about gluten-free living. Achieving this goal can become a source of pride for them.

And a gluten-free diet provides some advantages. Children cannot eat a lot of junk food, for instance, because it contains gluten. I've also found that most of my families whose children have celiac disease dine out less (and thus are more conscious of what they are eating). They also eat far fewer processed foods. Many families tell me that their kids' friends love to eat at their house, because they get such good homemade meals!

The secret of success to being gluten free is simple. Follow these three steps: (1) Be committed, (2) get educated, and (3) get organized. The purpose of this book is to help you achieve exactly that.

## Rx: Grab and Go Snacks!

All my patients with celiac are the most unhappy when they are without food—especially at parties, games, dances, or all such extracurricular events where having something to eat is part of the normal scene. But being hungry is a preventable problem. One of the biggest aspects of really sticking to a gluten-free diet is to organize yourself before the desire for food arises. The sure cure for being hungry is always packing and having gluten-free snacks on hand. You will find suggestions throughout this book about how to organize, as well as recipes for homemade snacks and lists of readily available prepared snacks.

There are two suggestions my patients tell me really help, and they're things teenagers should learn to do for themselves. It's good preparation for when they travel without their families or go off to college. First, pair any one daily act from your normal routine with something you need to do to maintain gluten-free living. For example, every time you brush your teeth in the morning, pack a gluten-free snack in your backpack. Another suggestion: Take advantage of technology to remind you. For example, set your smartphone, or calendar on your computer, to signal you to pack your gluten-free snacks.

## Doctor's Visit: Making the Most of the Time

When patients come to the doctor's office, they often leave behind their reasons for coming. Then, back at home, they recall the questions they didn't remember to ask. Physicians can diagnose disease and treat it, but they aren't mind readers. To make the most of the doctor visit, and to be a better advocate for yourself and your child, I suggest the following:

1. Bring a concise list of symptoms you would like to discuss with the doctor. Most doctor visits are limited, so the more efficiently you can convey what is going on, the more time you will have to discuss your concerns.

2. Bring copies of relevant lab work.

3. Don't be embarrassed! Doctors routinely discuss frank and personal topics, such as bowel movements, bad gas, soiling, and the like. (I often joke that gastroenterology is such a glamorous profession.) Doctors help best when they know what is going on.

4. Before you come to the office, make a list of your top three concerns.

5. Take notes, or ask your doctor to write out directions for you. If possible, sometimes it is helpful to have two adults in the room. An extra person can be helpful to play with the child if the child is very young or can simply provide another set of ears.

Take these measures each time, and I believe you will find your visits to the doctor more reassuring, rewarding, and informative.

# The Survey: Top Thirty Foods Kids Miss Most

As a chef, restaurateur, and mother, Carlyn had her own ideas of what kids like and want to eat, but she wanted some feedback from real teens. So before developing all the recipes and writing the cookbook, she and I conducted an informal survey of teens to get some idea about which foods they missed or would most miss on a gluten-free diet. The teens were Sarah's friends and classmates, and my patients. Below is an excerpt from the survey form. If you have any doubts about the foods your own teens like and/or miss, by all means, let them fill out the survey. You might be surprised.

First, here are the questions we asked:

1. What foods do you miss most on a gluten-free diet?

2. Holidays and parties can be lots of fun—if you don't have to watch what you eat. Please list the holiday and party foods that you miss on a gluten-free diet.

When the survey forms came back, we treated it like an election: The foods with the most votes won. Following is a list of the top thirty foods that our survey kids said they missed most. There are recipes for all of them in the cookbook except for foods that are seldom prepared from scratch at home and foods that are mostly purchased prepared and/or packaged, such as bagels, Goldfish and other crackers, Pop-Tarts, hot dogs (though we do have a recipe for buns), and pretzels. Prepared gluten-free versions or good mixes of some of these foods are available in stores or online (see "Don't Reinvent the Wheel," page 22).

The top thirty foods that our survey kids miss most on a gluten-free diet:

| | | |
|---|---|---|
| "Good" bread | Grilled cheese sandwiches | Cake (yellow/chocolate/ |
| Doughnuts | French fries | birthday) and cupcakes |
| Pancakes and waffles | Ranch dressing | Frosting |
| Cinnamon rolls | Chicken nuggets and fish sticks | Apple pie |
| Muffins | Pizza | Pumpkin pie |
| Coffee cake | Spaghetti/meatballs | Cookies (Chocolate chip/ |
| French toast | Linguine Alfredo | oatmeal/sugar) |
| Biscuits | Lasagna | Pudding (vanilla/chocolate) |
| Banana and pumpkin breads | Macaroni and cheese | |
| Chicken noodle soup | Gravy | |
| Hamburgers/cheeseburgers/ | Stuffing | |
| hot dogs/hot dog and | Barbecue (ribs/chicken/sauce) | |
| hamburger buns | Brownies | |

## Don't Reinvent the Wheel

Following are prepared gluten-free foods and mixes that Carlyn and Sarah's family have enjoyed eating and have had success preparing. Make a list of products that you try and like, and be on the lookout for new gluten-free products that are coming to market every month, it seems. One company is even reported to be developing a gluten-free toaster tart similar to Pop-Tarts. It's a good idea to call the manufacturers periodically to verify the gluten-free status of their products, since they may change the ingredients without notice.

### Prepared and/or Packaged Foods

Bell & Evans frozen breaded chicken breast nuggets

Dark Chocolate Dream 100% dairy-free almond dark chocolate bar

DeBoles rice lasagna (no boiling, oven ready)

Enjoy Life semi-sweet chocolate mini chips

Flamous falafel chips (original; spicy)

Glutino crackers, pretzels

Graham crackers: Enjoy Life, Schär, The Grainless Baker

Popchips barbeque potato chips

Rella Good Cheese Soyrella non-dairy mozzarella substitute

Rice Krispies gluten-free cereal

Simply 7 hummus chips

Snyder's of Hanover gluten-free pretzel sticks

Teese mozzarella vegan cheese alternative (for pizza)

Tinkyáda Pasta Joy brown rice pasta (long and short shapes)

Tofutti Sour Supreme and Better Than Cream Cheese (mozzarella flavor for grating and mozzarella and American cheese flavors in slices)

Trader Joe's ginger snaps

Trader Joe's organic brown rice penne pasta

Trader Joe's Snickerdoodle soft-baked cookies

Trader Joe's wheat-free toaster waffles

Udi's cookies (oatmeal raisin, chocolate chip)

Udi's muffins (double chocolate, blueberry)

Wellaby's classic cheese crackers

### Gluten-Free Mixes

Ad Hoc brownie mix

Ad Hoc waffle and pancake mix

Betty Crocker gluten-free cake mixes (devil's food and yellow)

Betty Crocker gluten-free chocolate chip cookie mix

Bisquick gluten-free pancake and baking mix

Bob's Red Mill Homemade Wonderful Bread Mix and Hearty Whole Grain Bread Mix (flour blend and single-variety gluten-free flours)

Chebe Original Cheese Bread Mix

King Arthur Flour gluten-free mixes: gluten-free flour, bread, cookies, brownies, cake, pancakes, and pizza crust

Kinnikinnick Foods angel food cake mix

The Really Great Food Company angel food cake mix

# GUIDE TO GLUTEN-FREE EATING AND COOKING

by Carlyn Berghoff

## The Gluten-Free Kitchen

While the right decision for our family was to become 100 percent gluten free, if you decide to be a house with dedicated gluten-free zones instead, see "The Gluten-Half-Free Kitchen," page 25. Remember, you will only have to do this once! To make the job seem less daunting, I divided the project into three areas:

Food Storage/Pantry
Refrigerator/Freezer
Equipment/Food Preparation
    Surfaces

## Food Storage/Pantry

I gathered all non-refrigerated foods and pantry items, read all ingredient labels, and made lists. Gluten-free foods went into one group; foods with gluten, into a second. Everything with gluten was carefully packaged and sent to a local food depository. Everything without gluten was relocated so that I could vacuum and wash with mild detergent all shelves and cabinets where shelf-stable food had been kept. I also washed all jars of gluten-free food. Gluten-free food packaged in boxes that could not be washed was transferred to new see-through plastic airtight stackable containers with lids and labeled.

Finally, I made a list of all the foods with gluten that needed to be replaced and shopped for gluten-free versions (examples: crackers, flour, canned goods). I replaced the contents of and reorganized my food pantry. It looked fabulous!

## Refrigerator/Freezer

I turned off the refrigerator/freezer, removed all the food, read ingredients, and made lists as I had done for the pantry. Of special note were foods that did not naturally contain gluten but could have been cross-contaminated (example: butter or peanut butter that had possibly been exposed to a knife that had touched bread). Because I could not donate the refrigerated foods with gluten to a food depository, I offered them to friends and relatives.

I removed all the shelves, washed down the entire refrigerator/freezer inside and out, and washed the shelves and replaced them. I washed all jars and plastic containers and frozen packages of gluten-free foods, replaced them on the refrigerator/freezer shelves, then turned on the refrigerator/freezer.

As with the pantry, I made a list of all the foods with gluten that needed to be replaced and shopped for gluten-free versions (examples: soy sauce, barbecue sauce, frozen baked goods). After that, it was a pleasure to open the refrigerator and freezer!

## Equipment/Food Preparation Surfaces

I divided all equipment into three categories:

Equipment that could be cleaned and kept
Equipment that needed to be replaced
New equipment that needed to be purchased

Equipment that could be cleaned and kept included the stand mixer, the food processor, the blender, the toaster oven, cooking pots, pans, and skillets, cooking spoons, whisks, spatulas, plastic containers with lids for refrigerator or freezer storage, and plastic cutting boards. I carefully inspected all used nonstick pans, spoons, spatulas, and cutting boards for surface cracks and discarded or donated anything that might be suspect. Gluten is sticky,

and sometimes washing will not remove it.

Equipment that needed to be replaced included the toaster, sieves, colanders, slotted spoons with small holes, rolling pins, wooden cutting boards, the bread machine, sponges, and dishcloths. I wasn't taking any chances of even the smallest trace of gluten remaining on those things.

New equipment included a dedicated bread machine, a french fry cutter, a doughnut pan, a hot dog bun pan, a hamburger bun pan, parchment paper, and a tape dispenser and several permanent markers. The latter are indispensable! I use them to label food for refrigerated or frozen storage. Simply stick a length of tape on the lid of the food container. Write the contents on it and date it. When the container is empty, peel off the tape and throw it away. If you don't already have parchment paper, I highly recommend you buy some. Parchment paper is crucial to gluten-free baking and cooking, and precut half sheets (16½ by 12¼ inches) are available in 100-sheet packages from King Arthur Flour. (www.kingarthurflour.com).

I meticulously washed and cleaned the stand mixer (turning it on its side and

using a cotton swab to rout out any flour residue in nooks and crannies), the blender and food processor housing, and the toaster oven inside and out. After scrubbing them by hand to remove any baked-in or stuck-on gluten particles, I put the mixer bowl and attachments, the blender jar and lid, the food processor work bowl and attachments, and the toaster oven tray in the dishwasher (in batches) and ran it through a complete cycle. The pots, pans, and skillets, cutting boards, cooking spoons, and utensils were also washed in the dishwasher, as were the plastic containers and their lids.

As for food preparation surfaces, all areas of the kitchen where food was cooked or prepared, such as countertops, the stovetop, and the microwave oven, were washed with a mild detergent, rinsed, and dried.

The entire process of switching to a 100 percent gluten-free kitchen took several days, and I did not (nor do I recommend anyone else to) do it alone. I had help from my kids and family members and friends. I felt as if I had a whole new kitchen and pantry.

## The Gluten-Half-Free Kitchen

If your household is not going to be 100 percent gluten free and some family members will maintain their unrestricted diet, then it is essential to create gluten-free zones in the three major areas of your kitchen—Food Storage/Pantry, Refrigerator/Freezer, and Equipment/Food Preparation Surfaces. To do this, you first need to do everything listed in "The Gluten-Free Kitchen" (page 23), except you do not need to throw out foods with gluten or cross-contaminated foods. Simply separate them. If this seems like an unreasonable amount of work just to create gluten-free zones, please remember that for celiac patients *one crumb of bread* can make them ill. General regulations for producers of gluten-free foods specify *no more than twenty parts gluten per million*.

## Suggestions for Creating Gluten-Free Zones

After cleaning out the food storage/pantry area, label all gluten-free food items clearly, and store them on a shelf *above* any wheat-based or gluten-containing foods. To be doubly safe from cross-contamination, store them in a dedicated bin or plastic box.

After cleaning out the refrigerator/freezer, label all gluten-free condiments, cheeses, and other foods, refrigerated or frozen, and place them on a top shelf by themselves. I suggest placing them on a large plastic tray that can be washed periodically. It is helpful to purchase gluten-free condiments in squeeze bottles that nobody else can dip into (ketchup, mustard, mayonnaise, jelly). And make firm rules: No double dipping of knives or spoons used on wheat bread or crackers into gluten-free condiments. Nobody else's food of any kind, including carryout and leftovers, can be stored on the dedicated gluten-free shelf.

For equipment/food preparation surfaces, I suggest purchasing all new cookware and utensils, including a toaster, and all new cutting boards and placing them in a plastic bin of their own. Use these for

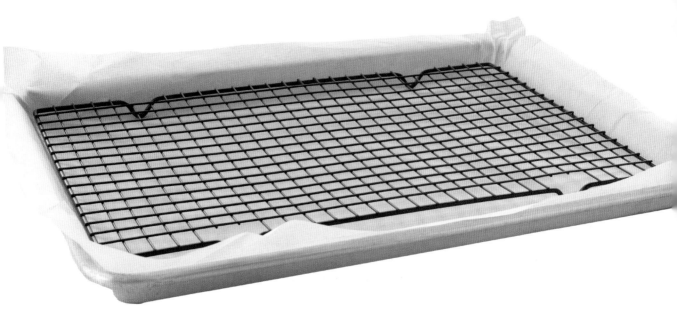

preparing gluten-free foods. You don't need an entire set of cookware, just a pasta pot, a nonstick skillet, a 2- or 3-quart pot with a lid, a colander, a bread knife, etc.

Prepare gluten-free foods first, on a freshly washed and dried surface, before you prepare other foods. Cook gluten-free foods first before you cook other foods, even when using a separate, dedicated pot.

After food preparation, clean up the counters carefully, using sponges or dishcloths that have not been used to wipe down counters where food with gluten has been prepared. Sponges and cloths are a source of cross-contamination. One of my friends uses paper towels because they can be used once, then thrown away. Wash all dishes and utensils in the dishwasher. And don't forget to wash your own hands, which can be a source of gluten cross-contamination.

## Grocery Shopping

Once the kitchen and pantry were set up and organized, I turned my attention to shopping. Taking my lists with me to the stores (you may find, as I did, that no one store has everything) helped me until I memorized them.

Reading labels is a must. At first, I found it time-consuming, but it has now become automatic. I still read labels: for any additive that may contain wheat; for the phrase "processed in a facility that also processes wheat, barley, rye," etc.; and for any change in the ingredients from the last time I purchased the food item. Manufacturers change their formulas all the time.

## Gluten-Free Foods

A gluten-free diet is not a diet of deprivation. There is an abundance of food safe to eat. Foods that are naturally gluten free include:

Minimally processed fresh (or frozen, defrosted) seafood, poultry, and meat, *without additives of any kind.*

Eggs, natural unprocessed cheese, milk (regular and lactose free), cream, yogurt, butter, and sour cream, *without additives of any kind except salt.*

Fresh fruits and vegetables, *without additives of any kind.*

Beans and lentils (including peanuts), dried and canned, *without additives of any kind except salt.*

Grains: rice (white, brown, red, black), corn (cornmeal, pop-corn, hominy, hominy grits), buckwheat (kasha), and wild rice.

Nuts: tree nuts such as almonds, Brazil nuts, cashews, chestnuts, hazelnuts, macadamia nuts, pecans, pine nuts, pistachio nuts, and walnuts.

Gluten-free flours (for cooking and baking) ground from beans, grains, legumes, nuts, and grains are numerous and include: acorn, almond, amaranth, arrowroot, artichoke, channa (a variety of chickpea), chestnut, chickpea (garbanzo, flour also called besan and gram, not to be confused with graham or wheat flour), coconut, corn flour, meal, and starch, dal (dhal, or split peas or beans from India ground into flour), fava bean, flaxseed, millet, potato starch and flour, quinoa, rice (white, brown, glutinous or sweet), sorghum (milo), soy, sweet potato, tapioca (manioc) starch and flour, and teff. Many of these are available in large supermarkets, as well as health- and whole-foods markets. But all are easily ordered on the Internet.

## Gluten-Full Foods

Foods with gluten that must absolutely be avoided include anything that contains:

Barley

Rye

Triticale

Wheat (durum, graham, kamut, semolina, spelt)

Malt, malt flavoring, malt vinegar (which is generally made from barley)

## Hidden Sources of Gluten

View all processed foods as questionable and read all their labels, because prepared foods are often hidden sources of gluten. For example:

Soy sauce contains wheat unless it is labeled gluten free, and then it is usually called "tamari."

Malt, made from barley, is not only in malt vinegar, but is used to flavor some cold and hot cereals.

Glue used on stamps, envelopes, and labels that you lick may have gluten. The same is true of self-stick labels and stickers.

Medications and cosmetics may contain gluten. Sometimes the pharmacist can tell you; other times you must call the manufacturer.

Among websites that list gluten-free medications and cosmetics is www.glutenfreedrugs.com.

## Gluten by Association

Basically, gluten by association is cross-contamination in any form. It can come from gluten on packaging, from additives, or from manufacturing in a facility that processes wheat. For example, french fries can be cooked with other foods that contain wheat and be cross-contaminated with gluten. Pre-grated packaged cheese can be coated with wheat starch to prevent clumping. Chocolate may be packaged on a conveyor belt also used for packaging wheat products. Gluten-free food products can be processed in any facility that also processes wheat products and pick up gluten from that environment. Try not to be overwhelmed, but do consult www.celiac.com for the very helpful "Unsafe Foods List." You can also get a free e-book from the University of Chicago Celiac Disease Center at www.cureceliacdisease.org under "Get the Facts."

# EATING OUT: SCHOOL, RESTAURANTS, AND AWAY FROM HOME

by Sarah Berghoff McClure

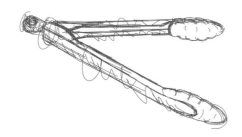

When you can't eat almost anything, anywhere, what do you say? When I was first diagnosed with celiac disease, I had to tell my friends, their parents, my teachers, and anyone at any place I'd be eating away from home.

Basically, I tell my friends that I am just allergic to wheat and gluten. Even though celiac disease technically isn't being allergic, it is too much of a hassle to explain what it really is. But I will tell my very close friends what celiac disease really is. I tell them my story and how sick I was.

I tell my friends' parents the same thing as I tell my friends, but I will go into more depth about how sick I was. They always ask me if I would ever sneak a bit of wheat, and I say, "No way! I was way too sick to ever want to touch it again!"

I explain to my teachers what celiac disease is, and I show them my doctor's notes (permission to use the microwave in the nurse's office, permission to use the restroom). But sometimes it's embarrassing to ask a male teacher for permission to use the restroom.

I do crew, and when I go to regattas, I tell the coaches how serious celiac disease is and how sick cross-contamination can make me. If, for example, they ask me if I can eat chicken breast, I have to ask if it was marinated in anything with wheat. And I also ask them to cook it for me on a piece of aluminum foil so it won't get cross-contaminated with other food.

Here are some things I learned that help me get through the day and stick to the diet. I hope they help you, too.

- Leftovers: Ask your mom to make extra whenever she is cooking dinner (especially over the weekend), so you will always have some left over to pack and reheat for lunch.
- Get two thermoses: Plastic containers for soup or drinks always wind up leaking. But if you get two wide-mouthed thermoses, you can use one for hot (soups, stews, hot sloppy leftovers) and one for cold (fruit, puddings). It really does keep cold, cold, and hot, hot. You can't reheat in the microwave, but you don't need to.

- Reheating food: Pack food to reheat in the microwave at school, or when you are out, in microwave-safe plastic containers with lids. Don't make the mistake of packing food in plastic bags.
- Plastic bags: Use them to wrap sandwiches, chips, cookies, vegetables like carrots and celery—anything that doesn't need a knife, spoon, or fork. They're quick to wrap and easy to open.
- Buy an insulated lunch bag: They're dorky looking, but you can find one you don't hate. They have places for an ice pack (always put one in) to keep things cold. They have waterproof linings that you can wash clean, and some have an outside pocket. Do not put your lunch in a brown paper bag. Stuff gets crushed and crumpled; paper bags are not big enough or strong enough.
- Always pack snacks: Nothing is worse than being hungry and not having food you can eat. And sometimes at school the lunch could be late, one of the last periods. If you get too hungry, you can't concentrate, and, like me, you may get hungry superfast.
- Always speak up: Tell the teachers that when you have to go to the bathroom, you really have to go. It may be awkward with male teachers, but it would be more awkward not to go.
- Pack your own cooler for a family trip: If you're going on a family trip (especially on an airplane where there's nothing you can eat) or to friends' houses for a long stay, pack a big cooler with everything you want to eat. For me, a good cooler has some turkey or ham, crackers, pretzels, fruit, jelly beans, hard candy, a big cupcake, cookies, sandwiches, dried fruit like raisins, peanut butter and gluten-free crackers, and gluten-free popcorn. Do not share your cooler with family members. You will get sick of packing it for them, they will eat your food, and you will have to lug it around. Let them get their own cooler.
- At restaurants, always ask what ingredients are in the food or drinks and how and with what they were prepared.

# SHARING TIPS
by Suzanne P. Nelson, MD, MPH

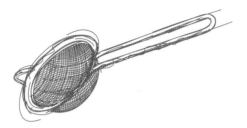

I keep a notebook in my office for kids and their families called "Sharing Tips for Gluten-Free Living." Most tips fall into eating out, at home, and abroad. So from the people who really know about the gluten-free lifestyle, my patients, come these tips:

- Gluten-free cards that you can print out in fifty-one languages are available at www.celiactravel.com. The cards explain what you can and cannot eat and also in which countries the language is spoken. The site also offers tips for gluten-free eating in planes and hotels and a wide variety of informative articles, for example, a gluten test kit for use at home and abroad.

- Leave gluten-free snacks at school with teachers for birthday parties and after-school dates.
- When shopping for gluten-free snacks, if it looks good, get it! If it tastes bad, don't sweat it. All kinds of yummy gluten-free foods are out there to try.
- When eating at Mexican restaurants, don't assume all nachos and tortilla chips are gluten free. Many are fried and can be cross-contaminated with gluten from the communal fryer. Some Mexican restaurants add flour to the cheese basin to act as an anticoagulating agent, so ask.
- Bring your own snacks everywhere, as well as your own food and cake to birthday parties.

- Order gluten-free-restaurant cards and carry them in your wallet (visit celiactravel.com). Before going to the restaurant, call ahead and talk directly to the chef. Or speak to the manager and ask to talk to the chef about cross-contamination and gluten-free items. Many chain restaurant companies have gluten-free lists. Contact them and see if they will send their lists.
- Asian restaurants are often a good gluten-free choice.

# Helpful Links

The Internet is a wonderful link to many helpful resources. Here are a few helpful sites:

www.cureceliacdisease.org The University of Chicago Celiac Disease Center is an authoritative resource for doctors and patients, and one of the best, most comprehensive sites available.

www.americanceliac.org American Celiac Disease Alliance is a national advocacy group for celiac disease and serves the needs of patients, researchers, food manufacturers, and others.

www.celiac.org The Celiac Disease Foundation is an excellent overall reference for celiac disease and has many lists: gluten-free foods, unsafe foods, gluten-free cosmetics and medications, gluten-free food manufacturers, and so on.

www.csaceliacs.info The Celiac Sprue Association site includes information on gluten-free cooking, a product listing, and Cel-Kids network.

www.glutenfreedrugs.com A frequently updated website authored by a clinical pharmacist that lists gluten-free drugs and phone numbers for some drug companies.

www.celiactravel.com has travel tips and free restaurant cards in fifty-one languages to download.

www.celiactravelguide.com has travel guides and tips, restaurant lists, and free dining cards to download.

www.gfreeconnect.com offers discounted gluten-free samples and discounts. It also has a list of gluten-free blogs.

# PART II

# The Cookbook

# The Best Place to Start

Do you hate or love to cook? Or do you fall somewhere in the middle? Do you order in a little or a lot? Do you eat out at restaurants a little or a lot? There is no right or wrong, no good or bad answer. But now that you must provide food for a family member with celiac disease, you probably need to make different choices. You don't want your kids to say what comedian Buddy Hackett said: "My mother's menu consisted of two choices: Take it or leave it."

If you don't want to cook, you can still order in gluten-free foods, and you can learn to make gluten-free choices at restaurants. Learning to cook gluten free is a more complicated process, and nobody learns it overnight. But once you learn it, it becomes a way of life, and cooking is much less expensive than ordering in or eating out.

The gluten-free ingredients are the biggest challenge: identifying them, finding them, buying them. After that, the cooking is just following directions.

I believe cooks come in two basic kinds: cooks (savory) and bakers (pastries/desserts). You will find recipes to suit both, but in my opinion, gluten-free baking is the bigger challenge. Many of the recipes in this book are quick and easy. Some take as little as 10 minutes. The baking recipes tend to require the most time and effort. The bottom line is that none of the recipes in this book are beyond the reach of any cook who can follow a straightforward recipe, and more than half of the recipes can be frozen, which means cooking once and eating twice.

I suggest you start with the easiest recipes and try to have fun. As our famous American cook Craig Claiborne said, "Cooking is at once child's play and adult joy. And cooking done with care is an act of love."

# Recipe Guidelines for Gluten-Free Cooking

All ingredients in every recipe must be completely gluten free.

- Read labels before you buy any ingredient, mix, or foodstuff.
- Consult www.celiac.org (the Celiac Disease Foundation website) for an alphabetical list of gluten-free beverages, prepared foods, ingredients and mixes, and medicines, cosmetics, and vitamins.
- Consult the lists "Gluten-Free Foods" (page 26) for safe ingredients, and "Gluten-Full Foods" (page 26) for ingredients to avoid.
- Check out "Hidden Sources of Gluten" (page 27) and "Gluten by Association" (page 27).
- Make sure your kitchen is either gluten-free (see "The Gluten-Free Kitchen," page 23), or has gluten-free preparation and food storage areas (see "The Gluten-Half-Free Kitchen," page 25).
- Measuring *exactly* is crucial in gluten-free cooking, and especially in baking. When you measure liquids, hold the measuring cup at eye level to make sure the ingredient is on the line. When measuring solids, fill a straight-sided measuring cup full and then use a long straight-edged spatula to level off the top. To get the correct amount of sticky ingredients such as honey and molasses, first spray the measuring cup or spoon lightly with vegetable oil cooking spray, then add the honey. It will slip off rather than cling.
- General ingredients: All onions are yellow onions. All eggs are large eggs. All ingredients such as bouillon cubes; beef, chicken, or vegetable broth; barbecue sauce; ketchup; mustard; and mayonnaise are gluten free.
- Special Ingredients: Many ingredients are especially useful in gluten-free cooking and baking. These include cider vinegar, dried egg whites, prepared refrigerated liquid egg whites, dried buttermilk powder, unflavored gelatin, and xanthan gum. The vinegar provides acid, which helps leavening. The egg whites, buttermilk powder, and gelatin help texture and structure. The liquid egg whites are especially useful for recipes such as bread that calls only for egg whites; using these eliminates leftover yolks. Xanthan gum is essential to add volume and moisture to gluten-free bread and baked goods. It is a natural carbohydrate, and it comes in powdered form. It is added in small quantities to gluten-free flour blends or as a recipe ingredient in recipes for gluten-free baked goods. A familiar brand is Bob's Red Mill. (There are other gums available for the same purpose, such as guar gum, ground from guar seeds; however, xanthan is my gum of choice.)

# Lactose Intolerance, Dairy Allergies, and a Gluten-Free Diet

Lactose intolerance involves digestion and is the inability to digest lactose, a sugar found in milk and milk products. Dairy allergy involves the immune system and a normally harmless substance (such as a dairy product) that the body reacts to as foreign. This releases chemical triggers that can result in inflammation. Allergies range in severity and, at their most intense, can result in anaphylactic shock.

When a person is newly diagnosed with celiac disease, they sometimes discover that they are also lactose intolerant. The problem may disappear when gluten is removed from the diet, or symptoms may continue for months or for as long as two years. Lactose-free milk and aged cheeses such as aged Cheddar, Parmesan, and Gruyère are sometimes well tolerated by lactose-intolerant people.

If, however, a person is allergic to dairy products, they will react to other substances in milk such as casein, a milk protein that can be found in some so-called "nondairy" cheeses. Only your physician can diagnose and advise on both of these conditions.

There are many products to use in gluten-free cooking that are marketed as nondairy or dairy free. Examples include rice- or soy-based cheeses, and nondairy beverages made from rice, soy, coconut, and almonds. Almost all are lactose free; however, some contain casein, a milk protein.

# Resources for Gluten-Free Products

Many gluten-free cooking ingredients are available at large supermarkets, and whole- and health-food markets. Almost all are available on the Internet. My experience ordering online has been positive thus far.

www.cfco.org
www.kingarthurflour.com
www.bobsredmill.com
www.celiac.com/glutenfreemall
www.nuts.com
www.glutenfree.com
www.amazon.com

# breakfast and bread

Gluten-Free All-Purpose Flour

White Sandwich Bread

Hot Dog Buns

Hamburger Buns

Berghoff Tastes-Like-Rye Bread

Fluffy Pancakes or Waffles

French Toast and French Toast Sticks

Drop Biscuits

Glazed Baked Doughnuts

Corn Bread

Almond-Sour Cream Coffee Cake

Pumpkin Bread Bars

Cinnamon-Raisin Bread and Cinnamon Buns

Cinnamon, Blueberry, or Chocolate Chip Muffins

Banana Bread Squares

Quiche

Breakfast Sausage Patties

All-Day Breakfast Sandwich

For many teens, and certainly for Sarah, breakfast is the most important meal of the day. According to the current medical and nutritional research, breakfast is the most important meal of the day for us all. It recharges the brain and body, maintains good health, and helps avoid obesity. As adults, we need breakfast to make us more efficient during the day, but kids need breakfast even more, because their growing bodies and developing brains depend upon regular eating. So when you look at the appetizing list of baked-goods recipes in this chapter, remember that a balanced breakfast also includes dairy products or dairy alternatives, cereal, and protein, such as eggs. The All-Day Breakfast Sandwich (page 71) has both bread (carbohydrates) and protein and needs only fruit for a completely balanced breakfast.

Many favorite breakfast foods rely on flour as an ingredient and baking as a technique. When it comes to gluten-free flours and baking, everything is different: the flour itself, the way doughs and batters are mixed, their consistencies, and their baking times. For all those reasons, it is not easy just to directly "convert" a recipe, one for one, for pancakes using wheat flour to one using gluten-free flour. The reason is simple: Wheat flour has gluten—the protein that traps gas (carbon dioxide) bubbles and allows the bread, biscuit, or pancake to rise with the aid of the steam created during baking—and leavening (yeast, baking soda, baking powder). When using gluten-free flours, the rising during baking must come from the steam and the leavening. There are no elastic gluten strands to capture and hold the gas.

Already prepared gluten-free flours, both single kinds and blends, are plentiful and available online. The recipes in this book were created for my own blend, Gluten-Free All-Purpose Flour (page 43). However, you may prepare any of them using your favorite gluten-free flour blend, or your own signature blend, as long as *there is xanthan gum (see page 37) in the mix*. If using another flour blend, the results may vary slightly in the finished recipe. The ratio of xanthan gum to gluten-free flour in my blend is roughly 1 teaspoon of xanthan gum to 1 cup of flour.

All gluten-free batters are thick and do not pour easily. The dough for gluten-free bread is especially thick and sticky, and you cannot knead it. For that reason, a bread machine for baking gluten-free bread is a great investment in saving time and labor, and also money, because store-bought gluten-free breads can be expensive. You can, of course, still bake a great loaf of gluten-free bread in a bread loaf pan in the oven. When mixing gluten-free doughs and batters, a stand mixer does the best job. You can use a hand-held mixer, and if the batter becomes so thick it begins to crawl up the beaters, simply scrape down the beaters and finish the mixing with a silicone spatula. If you are, as I once was, still wary of bread baking, then save the bread recipes and try them last.

It is entirely possible to bake fluffy, tender, delicious gluten-free bread, corn bread, pancakes, biscuits, coffee cake, muffins, and more—all the breakfast treats and sweets in this chapter. All of them can be frozen, which is a great time-saver for the cook and grab-and-go convenience for the teen and other family members.

# gluten-free all-purpose flour

## MAKES 12 CUPS

• • •

There are several all-purpose gluten-free flours on the market, some moderately priced, others costing $19 for 3 pounds. My blend is easy to mix, the ingredients are available at large supermarkets or online, and it is the only flour used in this cookbook. Though the final results may vary somewhat, you may substitute your favorite gluten-free flour as long as there is about 1 teaspoon of xanthan gum to 1 cup of flour. All you need to mix and store my flour blend is a large whisk and a 4-quart plastic food storage container with a tight-fitting lid. One batch of flour lasts one month at room temperature and may be frozen. White sorghum or quinoa flour provides protein; the sorghum is less expensive than quinoa. Try both and see which you prefer. Note that potato starch and potato flour are not the same; however, tapioca starch and tapioca flour, while differently labeled, are the same.

**2 cups brown rice flour**

**2 cups white rice flour**

**2 cups potato starch (not potato flour)**

**2 cups tapioca starch or tapioca flour**

**5 tablespoons xanthan gum**

**2 cups white sorghum flour or quinoa flour**

**2 cups cornstarch**

Measure each flour and starch by scooping or pouring into a 1-cup measuring cup, then leveling the cup with a straight-edged bench knife or long spatula. Scoop, measure, and level the xanthan gum by the tablespoon.

Place all the ingredients one by one *in the order listed* in a 4-quart container with a tight-fitting lid. After each addition, stir well from the bottom with a large whisk to mix. After adding the cornstarch, mix well from the bottom. Place the lid securely on the container. Shake and rotate the container to mix.

Store at room temperature for one month, or divide into three batches and place in self-sealing plastic bags. Label, date, and freeze.

**notes:** For easy and waste-free measuring, place a sheet of parchment paper on the counter. Scoop or pour the flour into the measuring cup and level the top. Place the measured flour in the container. Gather up the sides of the parchment paper and funnel the excess flour back into the flour package.

You will not use a complete bag of each flour for the batch. To preserve freshness, clip each bag securely, place in a self-sealing plastic bag, and freeze.

Gluten-free flours are listed in "Gluten-Free Foods" (page 26).

# Why Buy a Bread Machine?

Even though my restaurant makes thousands of loaves of bread a month from scratch, I have never been good at baking bread. I'm too impatient. I want instant cooking gratification. Imagine my chagrin when I had to provide gluten-free bread for my family and found that most gluten-free bread that I could buy was really expensive, had a short shelf life, crumbled at the touch of a knife, and tasted like sand or straw.

One day while shopping, I discovered a bread mix. It had instructions for making it in a bread machine. The rest is history. I bought a new bread machine (used machines can have cross-contamination from wheat bread) with a gluten-free cycle and tried my first package of gluten-free bread mix.

Magic! The bread machine does all the work. You put in the ingredients, close the lid, and a couple hours later, you have a beautiful, moist, tender loaf of gluten-free bread. I developed my own gluten-free flour blend and used it to make the bread my family loves, White Sandwich Bread (page 45).

Yes, you can mix, rise, and bake bread using a stand mixer or large-capacity food processor, bread pans, and a standard oven. And it will taste just as good. But for consistency, for freedom, and for everyday use, I highly recommend a bread machine.

# How to Use a Bread Machine

Manufacturers' instructions may vary, and you should always refer to those first, but here is the basic process for using a bread machine:

If the bread machine does not have a gluten-free cycle, use the regular basic white bread cycle. You need a cycle at least 2 hours long to develop fully risen, fully baked gluten-free bread.

The recipes in this chapter were developed for 2-pound loaves, so make sure your bread machine has a 2-pound capacity, but not larger. (Some large-capacity bread machines bake 2½- to 3-pound loaves.)

Remove the baking pan from the machine and insert the kneading blade(s) *before* you add any ingredients. (You don't want to get liquid or flour inside the machine.)

Put all the liquid ingredients in the baking pan first, the dry ingredients second. Then place the pan in the machine and lock it in according to machine directions.

After the machine begins to mix, open the lid once and scrape down all unmixed flour on the sides using a silicone spatula. Close the machine and let it go through the complete cycle.

After the bread is baked, remove the pan right away, using oven mitts, and invert it onto a rack. The kneading paddle should stay in the bread pan. If it is stuck in the bread, carefully slice it out with a plastic, not metal, knife, so as not to scratch the nonstick coating. Turn the bread, right side up, onto a rack to cool. Let cool to room temperature before slicing.

You can also select the dough or manual cycle on a bread machine to mix and proof bread dough to bake in other pans (hot dog bun, hamburger bun, and loaf). Remove the dough at the end of the cycle. Place it in your pan of choice, let it rise as needed, and bake.

# white sandwich bread

MAKES 1 (2-POUND) LOAF, 12 (½-INCH) SLICES,
8 HAMBURGER BUNS, OR 10 HOT DOG BUNS

• • •

This loaf bakes up white and fluffy, does not crumble, tastes fresh and sweet, and has a four-day shelf life at room temperature if tightly wrapped. It can be sliced, wrapped, and frozen as well. It is our family's go-to bread for sandwiches, and the dough is also used for Hot Dog Buns (page 48), Hamburger Buns (page 49), French Toast (page 54), Baked Stuffing (page 142), croutons, and bread crumbs. I do recommend a bread machine (see page 44), but you can also mix the dough in a stand mixer, in a food processor, or even with a large spoon in a bowl and bake it in the oven in a loaf pan. I recommend using prepared refrigerated liquid egg whites, so you don't wind up with extra yolks.

**1½ cups water**

**2 eggs, well beaten**

**2 egg whites, well beaten, or equivalent prepared refrigerated liquid egg whites**

**2 tablespoons canola oil**

**2 tablespoons honey**

**1 teaspoon cider vinegar**

**3½ cups Gluten-Free All-Purpose Flour (page 43)**

**1¼ teaspoons bread machine or instant yeast**

**1 teaspoon salt**

**Bread machine:** Remove the bread pan from the machine. Place the water, eggs, egg whites, oil, honey, and vinegar in the pan of the bread machine (make sure the kneading paddle is firmly attached before adding the liquid ingredients).

Add the flour, yeast, and salt. Replace the bread pan in the machine.

Start the machine, selecting the gluten cycle or white bread cycle.

While the machine is mixing, open the lid and, using a silicone spatula, scrape down the sides to remove any dry flour.

Close the lid and let the machine go through the complete baking cycle.

When the bread is finished, open the lid, remove the bread pan with oven mitts, and invert it to release the loaf. If the kneading paddle(s) is still in the loaf, slice it out carefully with a plastic, not metal, knife. Turn the bread, right side up, onto a wire rack and let cool to room temperature. Slice into ½-inch slices. Wrap the loaf tightly in plastic wrap.

**Stand mixer:** Place all the liquid ingredients in the work bowl of a stand mixer fitted with the flat beater attachment. Mix on low until well mixed. Add all the dry ingredients. Mix on low, scraping down the sides as necessary, until well mixed. Increase the speed to medium and mix for 5 minutes.

Leaving the beater attached, cover the entire bowl with plastic wrap and let the dough rise for 1 hour. After 1 hour, remove the plastic wrap and mix on low for 2 minutes. Remove and scrape down the beater attachment. Transfer the dough, using a silicone spatula, to a 9 by 5 by 3-inch nonstick loaf pan that has been sprayed with nonstick cooking spray.

Smooth the top of the loaf and spray lightly with nonstick cooking spray. Cover lightly with plastic wrap. Let rise in a warm place until doubled in size, about 45 minutes.

Preheat the oven to 375°F. Bake the fully risen bread until brown on top and cooked through and the internal temperature on an instant-read thermometer registers at least 200°F, about 35 minutes. Remove from the oven and remove the loaf from the pan. Let cool to room temperature on a wire rack. Slice into ½-inch slices. Wrap the loaf tightly in plastic wrap.

**Food processor:** Place all the dry ingredients in the work bowl of a large-capacity food processor (12 to 14 cups) fitted with the plastic blade. Pulse to mix. Place all the liquid ingredients in a large bowl or pitcher with a spout and mix well, so the honey doesn't cling to the bottom. With the machine running, pour the liquid ingredients into the feed tube. Process until smooth, about 1 minute.

Unlock the lid, but leave it on the machine. Cover the feed tube with the stopper. Let the dough rise until doubled in size, about 45 minutes. When the dough has doubled in size, lock the lid and pulse to deflate, less than 1 minute.

Using a silicone spatula, scrape the dough into a 9 by 5 by 3-inch loaf pan that has been sprayed with nonstick cooking spray and bake according to the stand mixer directions at left.

**Hand mixing:** Mix first the dry and then the liquid ingredients in an 8-quart bowl using a large spoon. Cover and let rise until doubled in size, about 45 minutes. Mix to deflate. Transfer the dough to a 9 by 5 by 3-inch loaf pan that has been sprayed with nonstick cooking spray and bake according to the stand mixer directions at left.

notes: Buy bread machine yeast or instant yeast in bulk (4-ounce jars or 8-ounce packages) rather than in individual packets. Once opened, store yeast in an airtight container in the freezer. You can use it right from the freezer.

All flour settles as it sits. So first fluff it with a large spoon, then spoon it into level-top measuring cups. Then level with a straight-edged spatula.

Do not refrigerate any baked bread. The refrigerator dries out all baked goods.

To freeze the bread, slice it into half-loaf sizes, or 2-slice packages for sandwiches. Wrap the packages first in plastic, then in foil. Label and date.

# hot dog buns

### MAKES 10 BUNS

• • •

**1 recipe White Sandwich Bread dough (see page 45)**

Spray a hot dog bun pan (holding 10 buns) with nonstick cooking spray. Also spray the inside of a self-sealing 1-gallon plastic bag. Place the dough in the bag. Cut a diagonal ¾-inch triangle off 1 corner. Squeeze the dough into the hot dog bun indentations, end to end, spraying the pan areas between the sides of the buns. Spray the buns lightly on top.

Let rise, lightly covered with plastic wrap, until doubled in size, about 45 minutes.

Preheat the oven to 375°F. Bake the buns until cooked through and brown on top, about 25 minutes. Remove from the pan. Let cool on a rack to room temperature. Slice vertically, but not all the way through, for hot dogs. Freeze leftover buns in a self-sealing plastic bag.

# hamburger buns

## MAKES 8 BUNS

• • •

**1 recipe White Sandwich Bread dough (see page 45)**

Spray a hamburger bun pan (holding 8 buns) with nonstick cooking spray. Also spray the inside of a self-sealing 1-gallon plastic bag. Place the dough in the bag. Cut a diagonal 1-inch triangle off 1 corner. Squeeze the dough in concentric spirals to fill each bun indentation. Spray the buns lightly on top. Let rise, lightly covered with plastic wrap, until doubled in size, about 45 minutes.

Preheat the oven to 375°F. Bake until the buns are cooked through and brown on top, about 30 minutes. Remove from the pan. Let cool on a rack to room temperature. Slice horizontally. Freeze leftover buns in a self-sealing plastic bag.

note: For pans holding fewer buns, bake in two batches, storing the dough in a resealable plastic bag in the refrigerator until ready to bake.

# berghoff tastes-like-rye bread

MAKES 1 (2-POUND) LOAF OR 12 (½-INCH) SLICES

• • •

For more than a century, people have been eating rye bread at the Berghoff Restaurant, and I have been eating it all my life. I couldn't live without it. So I developed a gluten-free version that is moist, tender, holds together for sandwiches, makes great toast, and is a great stand-in for the original. Teff flour is available online and in some supermarkets. The sweet, nutty flour is made from the seeds of a grass (*Eragrostis tef*) native to northeastern Africa.

**1½ cups water**

**2 eggs, beaten**

**2 egg whites, or equivalent prepared refrigerated liquid egg whites**

**2 tablespoons canola oil**

**2 tablespoons molasses**

**1 tablespoon cider vinegar**

**2 cups Gluten-Free All-Purpose Flour (page 43) or flour of choice with xanthan gum in the mix**

**1½ cups teff**

**2 tablespoons caraway seeds**

**2 teaspoons bread machine or instant yeast**

**1 teaspoon salt**

**Bread machine:** To a medium bowl, add the water, eggs, egg whites, oil, molasses, and vinegar. Beat well to mix and dissolve the molasses. Remove the bread pan from the machine. Pour the mixture into the pan.

Add the flour, teff, caraway seeds, yeast, and salt. Fit the pan into the machine. Select the gluten cycle or the white bread cycle.

When the machine begins mixing, lift the cover, and using a silicone spatula, scrape down the sides to remove any dry flour. Close the cover and let the machine go through the complete baking cycle.

When the cycle is finished, remove the pan from the machine with oven mitts, and invert it to release the loaf. If the kneading paddle(s) is still in the loaf, slice it out carefully with a plastic, not metal, knife, so as not to scratch the nonstick surface. Turn the

bread, right side up, onto a rack to cool. Let cool to room temperature before slicing.

**Stand mixer:** Place all the liquid ingredients in the work bowl of a stand mixer fitted with the flat beater attachment. Mix on low until well mixed. Add all the dry ingredients. Mix on low, scraping down the sides of the bowl as necessary, until well mixed. Increase the speed to medium and mix for 5 minutes.

Leaving the beater attached, cover the entire bowl with plastic wrap and let the dough rise for 1 hour. After 1 hour, remove the plastic wrap and mix on low for 2 minutes.

Remove and scrape down the beater attachment. Transfer the dough, using a silicone spatula, to a 9 by 5 by 3-inch loaf pan that has been sprayed with nonstick cooking spray. Smooth the top of the loaf and spray lightly with cooking spray. Cover lightly with plastic wrap and let rise in a warm place until doubled in size, about 45 minutes.

Preheat the oven to 375°F. Bake the bread until brown on top and cooked through, or until an internal temperature on an instant-read thermometer registers at least 200°F, about 35 minutes.

Remove from the oven; remove the loaf from the pan. Let cool to room temperature on a wire rack before slicing.

**Food processor:** Place all the dry ingredients in the work bowl of a large-capacity food processor (12 to 14 cups) fitted with the plastic blade. Pulse to mix.

Place all the liquid ingredients in a large bowl or pitcher with a spout. Mix well to dissolve the molasses. With the machine running, pour the liquid ingredients into the feed tube. Process until smooth, about 1 minute.

Unlock the lid, but leave it on the machine. Cover the feed tube with the stopper. Let the dough rise until doubled in size, about 45 minutes. When the dough has doubled, lock the lid and pulse to deflate, less than 1 minute.

Using a silicone spatula, scrape the dough into a sprayed 9 by 5 by 3-inch loaf pan and let rise and bake according to the stand mixer directions at left.

**note:** To freeze the bread, slice it into half-loaf sizes, or 2-slice packages for sandwiches. Wrap the packages first in plastic, then in foil. Label and date.

**variation:** Substitute 1 tablespoon of dill seeds for 1 tablespoon of the caraway, or substitute 2 tablespoons of dill seeds for all of the caraway.

# fluffy pancakes or waffles

MAKES 8 TO 10 (4- TO 5-INCH) PANCAKES OR 4 (7-INCH) WAFFLES

• • •

Forget most of what you know about making pancakes. Gluten-free-flour pancakes are neither mixed nor cooked the same way. This recipe delivers a fluffy, flavorful pancake that is not gummy (a frequent flaw of gluten-free pancakes). These pancakes take longer to cook at a lower temperature, and the batter should rest for 5 minutes before cooking. A nonstick square griddle pan gets the best yield. To make waffles, add extra oil or butter (see Variations). Beware bad pancake protocol: Do not flip more than once, and do not press down on pancakes with the spatula.

**1 cup Gluten-Free All-Purpose Flour (page 43) or flour of choice with xanthan gum in the mix**

**4 teaspoons sugar**

**2 teaspoons dried egg whites**

**1 teaspoon baking powder**

**½ teaspoon baking soda**

**½ teaspoon bread machine or instant yeast**

**½ teaspoon salt**

**1¼ cups plus 2 tablespoons milk (regular or lactose free) or nondairy alternative (almond, rice, soy)**

**1 egg, well beaten**

**2 tablespoons canola oil, melted butter, or nondairy alternative**

**Butter, pure maple syrup, jam, confectioners' sugar, or Cinnamon Sugar (page 53), for serving**

In a medium bowl, combine the flour, sugar, dried egg whites, baking powder, baking soda, yeast, and salt. Whisk to mix.

Add the 1¼ cups of milk, the egg, and the oil. Using a hand-held mixer, beat on medium speed just until the batter is smooth and no lumps remain. Do not overbeat. Important: Let the batter stand for 5 minutes. Stir in the 2 tablespoons of milk and mix until smooth.

Spray a 10- to 12-inch nonstick square griddle pan (smooth surface, no ridges) with nonstick cooking spray. Heat over medium heat until a drop of water sizzles and evaporates.

Ladle in the batter by the ¼ cupful. The pan should hold 4 pancakes comfortably. Cook until the bottoms are golden and the pancake edges begin to cook, about 2 minutes. Cook on medium, or if the pancakes brown too quickly, decrease the heat to medium-low. Using a spatula, turn each pancake and cook on the second side until lightly puffed and cooked through, 1 to 2 minutes.

Serve with butter and pure maple syrup, or spread with jam and dust with confectioners' sugar, or serve with butter and sprinkle with cinnamon sugar.

**variations:** **FOR BANANA PANCAKES,** slice ripe bananas into ⅛-inch-thick slices. Place 5 slices in each pancake as it cooks on the first side. Flip and cook until done.

**FOR STRAWBERRY PANCAKES,** substitute sliced ripe strawberries for banana slices.

**FOR CHOCOLATE CHIP PANCAKES,** stir ¼ cup of mini chocolate chips into the batter before cooking.

**TO MAKE WAFFLES:** Add 2 tablespoons of oil or melted butter to the pancake batter and cook on a nonstick waffle iron according to the manufacturer's instructions. The pancake batter recipe makes 4 waffles in an 8-inch diameter pan that makes 7-inch waffles, and the recipe can be doubled.

# cinnamon sugar

### MAKES ¾ CUP

• • •

Make this with the best, freshest cinnamon you can buy, and store it in an airtight jar for up to 2 months. I like a strong cinnamon flavor. You can decrease the cinnamon to 3 tablespoons for a milder flavor.

**½ cup sugar**

**¼ cup ground cinnamon**

In a small bowl, combine the sugar and cinnamon and whisk well to mix.

# french toast and french toast sticks

## MAKES 8 SLICES OR 24 STICKS

• • •

French toast is another of the breakfast foods kids surveyed missed most. It's great for bread that has dried past its prime. Cook whole slices of French toast or cut slices into thirds for French toast sticks to dip in syrup. Save the trimmed crusts and process in the food processor for bread crumbs. A 9 by 13 by 2-inch pan makes soaking the bread a breeze.

**4 eggs, well beaten**

**1 cup half-and-half or whole milk (regular or lactose free) or nondairy alternative (almond, rice, or soy)**

**2 tablespoons packed brown sugar**

**2 teaspoons vanilla extract**

**½ teaspoon salt**

**8 slices White Sandwich Bread (page 45) or bread of choice, crusts removed and reserved for bread crumbs (see Note)**

**Unsalted butter or dairy-free alternative, for serving**

**Pure maple syrup, for serving**

**Cinnamon Sugar (page 53), for serving**

In a 2-quart bowl, whisk the eggs, half-and-half, brown sugar, vanilla extract, and salt until the sugar is dissolved.

Pour the mixture into a 9 by 13 by 2-inch glass baking dish. For whole slices, fit as many bread slices as will lay flat in the dish to soak up the batter. For sticks, cut each bread slice into 3 equal pieces. Place in the dish to soak up the batter. After 5 minutes, turn the slices over carefully. Let soak for an additional 5 minutes.

Spray a 12-inch nonstick sauté pan with vegetable oil cooking spray and heat over medium heat until the pan is hot and a

drop of water sizzles immediately. Using a spatula, lift as many soaked bread slices or sticks as will fit, not touching, in the skillet. Sauté until browned on one side, about 4 minutes. Turn and cook until cooked through, an additional 4 minutes. Decrease the heat, if necessary, to prevent overbrowning. Meanwhile, place the remaining bread in the dish with the batter to soak. Cook as directed.

Serve at once or place on a parchment paper–lined baking sheet in a 250°F oven to keep warm. Serve with butter and maple syrup and a dish of cinnamon sugar.

note: To make bread crumbs, place the reserved bread crusts in a food processor fitted with the metal blade and process to make fine crumbs. Freeze in self-sealing plastic bags for soft bread crumbs. For dry bread crumbs, spread the crumbs on a parchment paper–lined baking sheet and bake at 325°F until golden and dry, 10 to 15 minutes.

# drop biscuits

MAKES 9 BISCUITS

• • •

Big, light, and fluffy, these biscuits are quick to mix, quick to bake and freeze, and reheat well. Be sure to let the dough stand for 5 minutes before baking. A ¼-cup cookie scoop works well and shapes even, round biscuits.

**2 cups Gluten-Free All-Purpose Flour (page 43) or flour of choice with xanthan gum in the mix**

**¼ cup sugar**

**1 tablespoon baking powder**

**½ teaspoon salt**

**½ cup (1 stick) butter or dairy-free alternative, plus more for serving**

**⅔ cup milk (regular or lactose free) or nondairy alternative (almond, rice, or soy)**

**1 egg, well beaten**

**Jelly, for serving**

Preheat the oven to 375°F. Line a half sheet pan (18 by 13 inches) with parchment.

In a medium bowl, combine the flour, sugar, baking powder, and salt. Whisk to mix well. Cut the butter into small pieces and add. Using your fingers, rub the butter into the flour until the mixture resembles coarse meal.

In a small bowl, whisk the milk and beaten egg well. Add to the flour-butter mixture, and stir until smooth and no lumps remain. Let rest for 5 minutes.

Scoop the dough by the ¼ cupful, 1 inch apart, onto the prepared pan. Bake until golden brown and puffed, 15 to 20 minutes.

Remove from the oven. Serve warm with butter and jelly.

note: To freeze the biscuits, let them cool to room temperature and freeze in a self-sealing plastic bag. Reheat in the microwave.

# glazed baked doughnuts

**MAKES 8 DOUGHNUTS**

• • •

Among the foods teens say they miss the most are doughnuts. This recipe makes cakelike doughnuts, tender on the inside, crisp on the outside. A nonstick doughnut pan works best, and the vanilla or chocolate glaze should be brushed on while the doughnuts are still hot. Vanilla glaze drizzled in a diagonal pattern on chocolate-glazed doughnuts, and chocolate glaze drizzled on vanilla-glazed doughnuts, looks nice. The doughnuts can be frozen. Just thaw them, glaze them, and serve.

**1 cup Gluten-Free All-Purpose Flour (page 43) or flour of choice with xanthan gum in the mix**

**½ cup sugar**

**¼ cup dried buttermilk powder**

**4 teaspoons dried egg whites**

**1 teaspoon baking powder**

**½ teaspoon baking soda**

**¼ teaspoon salt**

**2 eggs**

**¼ cup canola oil or melted butter or nondairy alternative**

**2 tablespoons water**

**1 tablespoon vanilla extract**

**Vanilla glaze or chocolate glaze (recipes follow)**

Preheat the oven to 375°F.

Spray a nonstick doughnut pan with nonstick cooking spray. Also spray the inside of a 1-gallon self-sealing plastic bag well with nonstick cooking spray. Cut a ¾-inch diagonal off 1 corner. (If the corner is cut too large, the doughnut yield will be less.)

In a 2-quart bowl, place the flour, sugar, buttermilk powder, dried egg whites, baking powder, baking soda, and salt. Whisk to mix well.

In a separate 2-quart bowl, place the eggs, oil or butter, water, and vanilla extract. Beat well with a handheld mixer.

Add the wet ingredients to the dry ingredients and mix to combine with a silicone spatula. Let the batter rest for 5 minutes.

Scrape the batter into the plastic bag, squeeze out the air, and seal. Push the batter toward the cut corner of the bag and, twisting the bag, pipe the batter into the doughnut pan, making a complete round. (Standard pans hold 6 doughnuts.) Bake for 10 minutes, or until the doughnuts are brown on top and cooked through.

Remove from the oven. Flip the doughnuts onto a cooling rack, then turn right side up. Place the cooling rack on a baking sheet or parchment paper to make cleanup easier when icing.

Repeat with the remaining doughnut batter.

Brush the doughnuts with the glaze while they are still warm. If using sprinkles, add now. Let the glaze dry until the doughnuts are completely cool. Wrap loosely and serve within 2 days, or wrap and freeze.

# vanilla glaze

• • •

1 cup confectioners' sugar

2 teaspoons vanilla extract

Pinch of salt

1 tablespoon milk (regular or lactose free) or nondairy alternative (almond, rice, soy), plus more as needed

Place the sugar in a small bowl. Add the vanilla extract and salt and the 1 tablespoon of milk and stir to mix. Add more milk only as needed. The glaze needs to be thin enough to spread with a pastry brush but thick enough to stick on the warm doughnuts.

# chocolate glaze

MAKES 1 CUP

• • •

1 cup confectioners' sugar

1 teaspoon vanilla extract

2 tablespoons unsweetened cocoa powder

Pinch of salt

1 tablespoon milk (regular or lactose free) or nondairy alternative (almond, rice, soy), plus more as needed

Place the sugar in a small bowl. Add the vanilla extract, cocoa, salt, and the 1 tablespoon of milk; stir well. Add more milk only as needed. The glaze needs to be thin enough to spread with a pastry brush but thick enough to stick on the warm doughnuts.

# corn bread

MAKES 1 (9 BY 9-INCH) PAN, 16 PIECES

• • •

Corn bread recipes fall into two broad categories: those that use straight cornmeal (southern), and those that combine cornmeal with flour and sugar (northern). My family favors the fluffier northern style, so my recipe uses gluten-free cornmeal and substitutes gluten-free flour for wheat flour. Corn bread is a snap to mix and bake, and it comes out of the oven hot and ready for butter and jam.

**1 cup cornmeal**

**1 cup Gluten-Free All-Purpose Flour (page 43) or flour of choice with xanthan gum in the mix**

**3 tablespoons sugar**

**1½ teaspoons baking powder**

**1 teaspoon baking soda**

**½ teaspoon salt**

**2 eggs, beaten**

**1⅓ cups buttermilk**

**3 tablespoons melted butter or nondairy alternative**

Preheat the oven to 425°F. Spray a 9 by 9-inch pan with nonstick cooking spray, line the bottom with parchment paper cut to fit, and spray lightly.

In a medium bowl, combine the cornmeal, flour, sugar, baking powder and soda, and salt. Whisk to mix.

In a separate small bowl, combine the eggs, buttermilk, and butter and whisk to mix.

Add the liquid ingredients to the dry ingredients and mix with a large spoon or silicone spatula until smooth.

Scrape the batter into the prepared pan. Let rest for 5 minutes. Bake for 20 minutes, or until a cake tester inserted in the middle comes out clean. Remove from the oven. Let cool for 5 minutes. Cut 4 by 4 into 16 squares. Serve warm or at room temperature.

variation: For a lactose-free version, substitute lactose-free milk for the buttermilk and add 1 teaspoon of cider vinegar to the milk before mixing with the dry ingredients.

# almond–sour cream coffee cake

## MAKES 1 (9 BY 13-INCH) PAN, 12 SERVINGS

• • •

This is my gluten-free version of the coffee cake I remember from my childhood, especially at my aunt Vita's house. There was always a pan of this cut into squares. It was my family's favorite before we became a gluten-free house, and it is still our favorite today. Please follow the recipe steps and measure exactly. Since the batter is really thick, it is important to level the batter so the cake bakes evenly.

1¼ cups sugar

8 ounces cream cheese, softened, or nondairy alternative

3 eggs

½ cup sour cream or nondairy alternative

2 teaspoons almond extract

1 teaspoon vanilla extract

2 cups Gluten-Free All-Purpose Flour (page 43) or flour of choice with xanthan gum in the mix

1 tablespoon dried egg whites

2 teaspoons baking powder

1 teaspoon baking soda

½ teaspoon salt

### streusel topping

⅔ cup packed brown sugar

⅔ cup Gluten-Free All-Purpose Flour (page 43) or flour of choice with xanthan gum in the mix

1 tablespoon ground cinnamon

1 cup sliced almonds

6 tablespoons melted butter or nondairy alternative

Preheat the oven to 350°F. Spray a 9 by 13 by 2-inch pan with nonstick cooking spray. Line the bottom with parchment paper cut to fit. Spray the parchment.

In a medium bowl, beat the sugar and cream cheese until the sugar is dissolved and the mixture is light. Add the eggs, one at a time, beating well after each addition, until the mixture is light and fluffy. Add the sour cream and extracts and beat well. Reserve.

In a separate medium bowl, combine the flour, dried egg whites, baking powder, baking soda, and salt. Whisk to mix well.

Beat the dry ingredients into the cream cheese mixture in 3 batches, beating only until mixed. Use the mixer on the first 2 batches, then scrape the beaters and mix the remaining dry mixture in with a silicone spatula. The batter will be quite thick.

Spoon the batter into the prepared pan. Oil a silicone spatula lightly, then spread the batter to the edges of the pan and level the top as smoothly as possible. Let rest while making the streusel.

To make the streusel: In a medium bowl, combine the brown sugar, flour, and cinnamon. Whisk to mix well. Add the almonds and stir to mix well. Drizzle on the melted butter and stir so the streusel is evenly moistened.

Sprinkle the streusel topping evenly over the cake batter. Let rest for 5 minutes. Bake until a wooden pick inserted in the center comes out clean, about 35 minutes. Remove from the oven and place on a rack to cool. When cool, cut 3 by 4 for 12 pieces.

**variations:** Omit the almonds from the streusel topping and the almond extract from the cake batter. Increase the vanilla extract to 2 teaspoons.

Substitute finely chopped pecans or walnuts for the almonds in the streusel topping and omit the almond extract from the cake batter. Increase the vanilla extract in the batter to 2 teaspoons.

# pumpkin bread bars

**MAKES 1 (9 BY 13-INCH) PAN, 18 BARS**

• • •

Pumpkin bread was up with banana bread on the list of foods kids surveyed missed the most. Like banana bread, pumpkin bread in a loaf shape takes a long time to bake and gluten-free flours perform better with shorter baking times. This recipe produces a perfect pumpkin bread flavor and texture when baked in a familiar glass 9- by 13 by 2-inch pan and cut into bars. Be sure to spread and level the batter in the pan before baking.

½ cup (1 stick) butter, softened, or nondairy alternative

1⅓ cups packed brown sugar

4 eggs

1 (15-ounce) can pumpkin (not pie mix) (2½ cups)

2 teaspoons vanilla extract

2½ cups Gluten-Free All-Purpose Flour (page 43) or flour of choice with xanthan gum in the mix

2 tablespoons dried egg whites

1 tablespoon pumpkin pie spice

2 teaspoons baking powder

1 teaspoon baking soda

¾ teaspoon salt

Confectioners' sugar or Vanilla Sugar (recipe follows), for garnish

Preheat the oven to 350°F. Spray a 9 by 13 by 2-inch (preferably glass) baking pan with nonstick cooking spray. Line the bottom with parchment paper cut to fit. Spray the paper.

In a medium bowl, beat the butter until light. Add the brown sugar and beat until smooth and fluffy. Add the eggs, one at a time, beating well after each addition, until light and fluffy. Add the pumpkin and vanilla extract and beat to mix.

In a separate medium bowl, combine the flour, dried egg whites, pumpkin pie spice, baking powder, baking soda, and salt and whisk to mix.

Add the dry ingredients in batches to the pumpkin mixture, mixing well with a large spoon. Scrape the sides and bottom of the bowl with a silicone spatula as needed. Scrape the batter into the prepared pan with a silicone spatula. Spread the batter to the edges of the pan and level, using an oiled silicone spatula or oiling the palms of your hands and patting level.

Bake for 30 to 35 minutes, until a wooden pick inserted in the center comes out clean. Remove from the oven. Set on a rack to cook. When cool, cut 3 by 6 for 18 bars. Before serving, dust the bars with confectioners' sugar or vanilla sugar. Wrap leftover individual bars in plastic wrap, label, and freeze for up to 30 days.

# vanilla sugar

• • •

Burying one or two vanilla beans in a 2-pound container of confectioners' sugar for a couple of weeks produces a fragrant topping for cookies, cakes, pancakes, French toast, brownies, quick breads, and bars. It can be kept going indefinitely by adding additional sugar and the occasional vanilla bean.

**2 pounds confectioners' sugar**

**2 vanilla beans**

Place the confectioners' sugar in an airtight container. Bury the vanilla beans in the sugar. Seal. Let rest undisturbed for at least 2 weeks before using.

# cinnamon-raisin bread and cinnamon buns

**MAKES 1 (2-POUND) LOAF OR 12 (3 BY 3¼-INCH) BUNS**

• • •

Cinnamon bread and cinnamon buns were listed often on our survey of foods kids missed the most. Gluten-free bread dough can't be kneaded by hand, rolled out, spread with cinnamon sugar, and rolled into a log and baked, creating the signature "swirl." This bread is a satisfying stand-in, makes great toast, and when baked into square buns and frosted, is even a good replacement for cinnamon buns.

**1½ cups water**

**2 eggs, beaten**

**2 egg whites**

**¼ cup melted butter or nondairy alternative**

**1 teaspoon cider vinegar**

**1 teaspoon vanilla extract**

**3½ cups Gluten-Free All-Purpose Flour (page 43) or flour of choice with xanthan gum in the mix**

**⅓ cup packed brown sugar**

**1 tablespoon ground cinnamon**

**2 teaspoons bread machine or instant yeast**

**1 teaspoon salt**

**½ cup raisins**

**Bread machine:** Remove the pan from the bread machine. Attach the kneading paddle(s) securely. Place the water, eggs, egg whites, butter, vinegar, and vanilla extract in the pan. Add the flour, brown sugar, cinnamon, yeast, salt, and raisins. Place the pan back in the machine.

Start the machine selecting the gluten-free cycle or white bread cycle. While the machine is mixing, open the lid and, using a silicone spatula, scrape down the sides to remove any dry flour. Close the lid and let the machine go through the complete baking cycle.

When the bread is finished, open the lid and remove the pan from the bread machine with oven mitts and invert it to release the loaf. If the kneading paddle(s) is still in the loaf, slice it out carefully with a plastic, not a metal, knife. Turn the loaf, right side up, onto a wire rack to cool. Let cool to room temperature.

Slice into ½-inch slices. Wrap tightly in plastic wrap. The bread will keep for 3 to 4 days at room temperature.

**Stand mixer:** Place all the liquid ingredients in the work bowl of a stand mixer fitted with the flat beater attachment. Mix on low until well mixed. Add all the dry ingredients. Mix on low, scraping down the sides as necessary, until well mixed. Increase the speed to medium and mix for 5 minutes.

Leaving the beaters attached, cover the entire bowl with plastic wrap and let the dough rise for 1 hour. After 1 hour, remove the plastic wrap and mix on low for 2 minutes.

Remove and scrape down the beaters. Transfer the dough, using a silicone spatula, to a 9 by 5 by 3-inch nonstick loaf pan that has been sprayed with nonstick cooking spray. Smooth the top of the loaf and spray lightly with nonstick cooking spray. Cover lightly with plastic. Let rise in a warm place until doubled in size, about 45 minutes.

Preheat the oven to 375°F. Bake the fully risen bread until brown on top and cooked through, or until an internal temperature on an instant-read thermometer registers at least 200°F, about 35 minutes.

Remove from the oven; remove the loaf from the pan. Let cool to room temperature on a wire rack.

**Food processor:** Place all the dry ingredients except for the raisins in the work bowl of a large-capacity food processor (12 to 14 cups) fitted with the plastic blade. Pulse to mix. Place all the liquid ingredients in a large bowl with a spout or a pitcher and mix well. With the machine running, pour the ingredients into the feed tube. Process until smooth, about 1 minute.

Unlock the lid, but leave it on the machine. Cover the feed tube with the stopper. Let rise until doubled in size, about 45 minutes. When the dough has doubled, lock the lid and pulse to deflate, less than 1 minute.

Using a silicone spatula, transfer the dough to a bowl. Add the raisins and mix well. Scrape the bread into a 9 by 5 by 3-inch loaf pan that has been sprayed with nonstick cooking spray and bake according to the stand mixer directions.

note: To freeze the bread, slice it in half-loaf sizes, or 2-slice packages for sandwiches. Wrap first in plastic, then in foil. Label and date.

variation: For cinnamon buns, use a bread machine set on "Manual" or the dough cycle and remove the dough at the end of the cycle. Or use a stand mixer or food processor to mix the dough.

Let the dough rise once, then mix to deflate. Scrape the dough into a 9 by 13 by 2-inch baking pan that has been sprayed with nonstick cooking spray and lined on the bottom with parchment paper cut to fit. Let rise until doubled. Rising time will vary between 20 and 25 minutes (for the bread machine dough) and 45 minutes for the dough mixed in the stand mixer or food processor. Bake at 375°F until cooked through, 35 to 40 minutes.

Remove from the oven, and let cool completely. Frost in the pan with Vanilla Glaze (page 58), letting the glaze drip down the sides of the bread. Let sit until the glaze hardens. Cut 3 by 4 into 12 pieces.

# cinnamon, blueberry, or chocolate chip muffins

**MAKES 8 CINNAMON, 10 BLUEBERRY, OR 9 CHOCOLATE CHIP MUFFINS**

• • •

To make up for the lack of gluten in the gluten-free flour in this recipe, I add protein from dried egg whites and unflavored gelatin to create a texture that is fluffy and tender. These muffins freeze well and taste great slathered with butter, whether right from the oven or at room temperature. Pull or tear the muffins apart rather than cutting them with a knife.

**1 cup Gluten-Free All-Purpose Flour (page 43) or flour of choice with xanthan gum in the mix**

**⅓ cup sugar**

**2 teaspoons dried egg whites**

**2 teaspoons unflavored gelatin**

**2 teaspoons baking powder**

**¼ teaspoon salt**

**½ cup whole milk (regular or lactose free) or nondairy alternative (almond, rice, or soy)**

**2 eggs**

**2 tablespoons canola oil**

**1 teaspoon vanilla extract**

**Cinnamon Sugar (page 53) or plain sugar, for dusting**

Preheat the oven to 400°F. Spray a 12-cup metal muffin pan with nonstick cooking spray. Line with paper muffin cups. Spray the cups.

In a medium bowl, place the flour, sugar, dried egg whites, gelatin, baking powder, and salt. Whisk well to mix. Reserve.

In a separate medium bowl, place the milk, eggs, oil, and vanilla extract. Beat well with a handheld mixer.

Add the dry mixture to the milk-egg mixture and beat to mix. If the batter becomes too thick for the mixer, scrape the beaters and use a large spoon to mix well. Important: Let the batter rest for 10 minutes before baking.

Fill each of 8 muffin cups with ¼ cup of batter. A 2-ounce cookie scoop works best. Otherwise scoop out ¼ cup and level.

Sprinkle each of the tops with ½ teaspoon of cinnamon sugar. Bake for 20 minutes, or until the muffins are golden brown on top and cooked through. Remove the muffin pan to a wire rack and let cool for 5 minutes, then transfer the muffins to a rack to cool.

Serve immediately, or let cool to room temperature and freeze in self-sealing plastic bags. To serve, thaw to room temperature and warm for 15 to 20 seconds in the microwave.

**variations:** **FOR BLUEBERRY OR CHOCOLATE CHIP MUFFINS,** decrease the baking powder to 1½ teaspoons, add ½ teaspoon of baking soda, and fold in ¾ of cup fresh blueberries, drained and patted dry, or ¾ cup of mini chocolate chips. Omit the sugar topping, and bake as directed.

# banana bread squares

## MAKES 1 (9 BY 9-INCH) PAN

• • •

Banana bread was high on the survey list of foods kids missed the most on a gluten-free diet. Gluten-free banana bread in a loaf pan takes a long time to cook, just like the wheat flour versions. But baked in a 9 by 9-inch square pan, it bakes quickly and comes out light and tender. For the best flavor, make sure to use super-ripe bananas. It is important to level the batter, because it is thick.

¼ cup (½ stick) unsalted butter, softened, or nondairy alternative

⅔ cup packed brown sugar

2 eggs

1 teaspoon vanilla extract

1⅓ cups smoothly mashed very ripe bananas (about 3)

1⅓ cups Gluten-Free All-Purpose Flour (page 43) or flour of choice with xanthan gum in the mix

2 teaspoons dried egg whites

1 teaspoon ground cinnamon

1 teaspoon baking powder

1 teaspoon baking soda

¾ teaspoon salt

¼ teaspoon ground allspice

Preheat the oven to 350°F. Spray a 9 by 9-inch baking pan with nonstick cooking spray. Line the bottom with parchment paper cut to fit. Spray the parchment with cooking spray.

In a medium bowl, beat the butter and brown sugar until very smooth and fluffy. Add the eggs, one at a time, beating well after each addition, until light and fluffy. Add the vanilla extract and bananas and beat well.

In a separate medium bowl, whisk the flour, dried egg whites, cinnamon, baking powder, baking soda, salt, and allspice to mix.

Add the dry ingredients in batches to the banana mixture, beating well after each addition. The batter will get very thick, so beat only enough to mix well.

Scrape the banana batter into the prepared pan with a silicone spatula. Pat smooth and level with oiled palms or a lightly oiled silicone spatula. Bake for 30 to 35 minutes, until a wooden pick inserted in the center comes out clean. Remove from the oven. Let cool on a rack. When cool, cut 3 by 4 for 12 bars.

variations: Dust the top with confectioners' sugar.

Frost the top with Vanilla Glaze (page 58).

# quiche

• • •

My family loves quiche, so I prepare it in many ways. I use a 9-inch glass pie pan rather than the traditional straight-sided quiche pan, because it makes preparation so much easier. Cheese and bacon quiche is our favorite, but there are many other tempting variations to try.

**1 Pat-in-the-Pan Pie Crust (page 168), prebaked**

**3 eggs, beaten**

**1 cup heavy cream or half-and-half**

**¼ teaspoon salt**

**1 cup grated Swiss cheese (4 ounces)**

**¼ cup finely chopped crisp bacon (4 slices)**

Preheat the oven to 375°F. Set the pie plate with the prebaked crust on a half sheet pan (18 by 13 inches).

In a medium bowl, whisk the eggs, cream, and salt until smooth. Reserve.

Sprinkle the cheese evenly on the bottom of the pie crust. Sprinkle the bacon evenly on the cheese.

Gently pour in the egg-cream mixture, scraping the bowl with a silicone spatula.

Bake for 35 minutes, or until the quiche is slightly puffed and golden. Remove from the oven and set on a wire rack to cool. Serve warm or at room temperature, cut into 8 wedges.

variations: **FOR A NONDAIRY QUICHE,** substitute rice or soy milk for the cream, and nondairy cheese for the Swiss.

**FOR CHEDDAR-HAM QUICHE,** substitute Cheddar cheese for the Swiss, and finely diced ham for the bacon.

**FOR SPINACH QUICHE,** use the cheese, but omit the bacon, and add 1 cup of squeezed-dry chopped spinach (either cooked fresh or defrosted frozen).

**FOR VEGETABLE QUICHE,** use the cheese, but substitute 1 cup of cooked chopped vegetables of choice (such as sliced mushrooms and chopped jarred red peppers, or corn kernels and green beans, or asparagus and red peppers).

Substitute blue, Cheddar, feta, jalapeño Jack, mozzarella, or provolone for the Swiss cheese.

# breakfast sausage patties

**MAKES 6 PATTIES**

• • •

Several gluten-free breakfast sausages are available; however, it is so easy and economical to mix and freeze your own. Homemade breakfast sausage is preservative- and MSG-free, low in sodium, and tastes great. Why not double the recipe and freeze the patties for another breakfast?

**1 recipe Basic Burger using turkey (page 103)**

**1 teaspoon rubbed sage**

**1 teaspoon dried thyme**

**1 teaspoon garlic powder**

**1 teaspoon onion powder**

**½ teaspoon liquid smoke**

**⅛ teaspoon cayenne pepper (see Notes)**

Place the turkey burger mixture in a 2-quart bowl. Stir in all the seasonings. Mix well. Form into ½-inch-thick patties and sauté in a 12-inch sauté pan over medium heat until browned on one side, about 6 minutes. Flip and sauté until cooked through, another 5 to 6 minutes.

notes: The ⅛ teaspoon of cayenne pepper makes a lightly spicy sausage burger. If you like sausage hot, increase the cayenne to ¼ or ⅓ teaspoon.

You can shape the patties, lay them flat on a parchment paper–lined 9 by 12-inch tray, and put them in the freezer. When frozen solid, transfer to a self-sealing plastic bag, date, and label. Defrost and cook according to the recipe.

# all-day breakfast sandwich

MAKES 6 SANDWICHES

• • •

When time is short, work has been hard, and I get home late and tired, I always serve breakfast for dinner: pancakes, eggs, toast, and our favorite, the breakfast sandwich. Before we became a gluten-free household, I used to make this and serve it on croissants. Now, I think it is even better on toasted White Sandwich Bread (page 45).

**12 slices bacon**

**12 slices White Sandwich Bread (page 45) or bread of choice, toasted**

**6 servings scrambled eggs**

**Salt**

**6 slices aged Cheddar or Gruyère cheese or nondairy alternative**

Preheat the oven to 350°F. Arrange the bacon on a broiler pan or rimmed baking sheet and bake for 20 minutes, or until it has reached the desired degree of doneness. Transfer with tongs to paper towels.

Place 6 slices of the toasted bread on a clean, dry surface. Evenly distribute the scrambled eggs over the toast. Season lightly with salt. Top each with a slice of cheese and 2 pieces of bacon. Finish each sandwich with a slice of toasted bread. Cut each sandwich in half.

Chapter 2

# starters and snacks

Hummus

Spinach Dip

Green Onion Dip

White Bean Dip

Sweet Potato Fingers with Marshmallow Dip

Nachos

Quesadillas and Beyond

Ham and Cheese Roll-Ups

Sarah's Spring Rolls

Snacks are critical to fill what I call the hunger gap, the time after school or before dinner. Then there are the after-dinner homework or television munchies, or the I-didn't-really-dig-dinner-what-else-have-you-got?

Adults enjoy snacks, but nutritional research suggests that teens actually need snacks because they feel hungry a lot (especially celiac kids) and they need the extra nutrients to help their adolescent bodies to grow. Of course, high-sugar, empty-calorie snacks are not the kind recommended. While kids can grab gluten-free chips or popcorn and fresh fruit, they are easily bored by the same few treats. I try to prepare snacks that have some nutritional value, a lot of flavor, and a little imagination. And I like to make snacks that can double as first courses or appetizers on a buffet. The snacks in this chapter can also travel well to school for lunch or for after-school events and to picnics.

The four dips can be mixed in the food processor in about the same number of minutes and served with chips, crackers, or vegetable crudités. Once you have the basic idea of a food-processor dip, don't stop with these four recipes, but experiment and create your own. You could try cream cheese, peanut butter, and jelly; cream cheese, ripe avocado, and salsa; cream cheese, slivered almonds, cinnamon, and honey; or kidney beans and bacon bits.

Ham and Cheese Roll-Ups (page 83) are like sandwiches without the bread or wraps without the wrapping. Nachos, a traditional favorite, are even easier to prepare when you make them plate by plate. Spring rolls, a standard Thai restaurant appetizer, are surprisingly simple to make by using an ingredient assembly line. Spring roll wrappers are available in the Asian section of large supermarkets, at Asian markets, and online. Some are made from wheat flour, so read the label. The only ingredients should be rice flour and water.

Quesadillas, made from corn tortillas, open up an entire world of new snacks. Quesadillas and Beyond (page 82) includes recipes for familiar cheese quesadillas, and more creative variations including a quesadilla pizza and a dessert quesadilla. Cinnamon-scented Sweet Potato Fingers with Marshmallow Dip (page 79) can double as a snack or as a vegetable side at dinner.

# hummus

MAKES 1½ CUPS

• • •

This no-tahini hummus is lightning fast to prepare and costs a fraction of prepared hummus. Make it fresh and serve it as a dip for chips or vegetables; a spread for bruschetta or crackers; in place of butter on toast; or to spread on cheese quesadillas before grilling.

**1 (15½-ounce) can garbanzo beans (chickpeas), drained and juice reserved**

**1 medium garlic clove, quartered**

**Juice of 1 lemon**

**½ teaspoon salt**

**¼ cup olive oil**

**Chopped flat-leaf parsley, for garnish**

Place the drained garbanzo beans in a colander and rinse well under cold water. Drain well.

Place the beans, garlic, lemon juice, and salt in the work bowl of a food processor fitted with the metal blade and process until finely ground, stopping the machine and scraping down the sides of the bowl as necessary.

With the motor running, pour the olive oil through the feed tube. Process to a smooth puree, about 2 minutes. If the dip is too thick, add the reserved liquid from the can 1 tablespoon at a time.

Transfer to a small bowl. Garnish with the parsley. Serve immediately or refrigerate, covered, for up to 4 days.

**variations:** **FOR A BOOST IN FLAVOR,** add ⅛ teaspoon of ground cloves or allspice.

**FOR RED PEPPER HUMMUS,** add ¼ cup of chopped well-drained jarred roasted red peppers in water.

**FOR TOMATO HUMMUS,** add 2 tablespoons of tomato paste.

# spinach dip

• • •

Frozen chopped spinach is at the top of my list of convenience foods. I use it in Creamed Spinach (page 144) and this family favorite. It's great with taco chips, rice chips, or other gluten-free chips, or with vegetable crudités. You can also use it to stuff celery. It is important to squeeze the spinach as dry as possible and also to drain the jarred red peppers well to keep excess liquid from spoiling the creaminess of the dip.

**1 (10-ounce) package frozen chopped spinach, thawed and squeezed dry**

**½ cup sour cream or nondairy alternative**

**½ cup mayonnaise**

**¼ cup finely chopped well-drained jarred roasted red bell peppers**

**½ teaspoon garlic powder**

**½ teaspoon onion powder**

**¼ teaspoon salt**

**⅛ teaspoon cayenne pepper**

In a medium bowl, mix all the ingredients well until very creamy. Cover and refrigerate for up to 4 days.

variation: For a smoother dip, place the squeezed spinach on a cutting board and chop finely before mixing with the other ingredients.

# green onion dip

• • •

This dip has some zip to it and works well with the usual chips and crudités. It also is good spread thinly on ham sandwiches and boosts grilled cheese sandwiches and panini. Make sure to soften the cream cheese to room temperature for easy mixing.

**8 ounces cream cheese or nondairy alternative**

**½ cup sour cream or nondairy alternative**

**¾ cup minced green onions, or ½ cup minced green onions and ¼ cup minced yellow onion**

**½ teaspoon finely grated lemon zest**

**½ teaspoon salt**

**¼ teaspoon celery salt**

In a medium bowl, mix all the ingredients until smooth and creamy. Cover and refrigerate for up to 4 days.

# white bean dip

MAKES 2 CUPS

• • •

With fast food off the table at home, I found new snacking options, and dips are among the easiest and best snack foods. They are also nourishing and healthful. This high-protein bean dip has a smooth texture and rich flavor. It's great with chips, crackers, or crudités. You can also use it in place of chili or refried beans on nachos.

**2 (14-ounce) cans white beans (cannellini, Great Northern), drained and rinsed**

**¼ cup packed crumbled feta cheese**

**⅛ cup extra virgin olive oil**

**⅛ cup fresh lemon juice**

**2 teaspoons dried parsley**

**1 teaspoon garlic powder**

**1 teaspoon onion powder**

**½ teaspoon finely grated lemon zest**

**¼ teaspoon salt**

Place all the ingredients in the work bowl of a food processor fitted with the metal blade. Pulse until very finely chopped, scraping down the sides of the bowl as needed. Process until smoothly pureed. Refrigerate, covered, for up to 4 days.

suggested uses: **MAKE A HOT LAYERED DIP:** Layer taco chips, the bean dip, salsa, and grated cheese in a small microwave-safe bowl. Heat until the cheese is melted. Garnish with chopped green onions or sliced pimiento-stuffed green olives.

**MAKE A MEXICAN PIZZA:** Layer a corn tortilla with the bean dip, salsa, and grated cheese. Bake or microwave until the cheese is melted and the pizza is hot.

**MAKE QUESADILLAS:** Spread the bean dip on a corn tortilla, sprinkle with grated cheese, and top with a second tortilla. Microwave or fry in a nonstick skillet until the cheese melts and the bean dip is hot. Cut into triangles to serve.

# sweet potato fingers with marshmallow dip

## MAKES 4 TO 6 SERVINGS

• • •

Oven baked, naturally sweet, and cinnamon flavored, these sweet potato fingers are a good dipping snack with Marshmallow Fluff, or a great side dish drizzled with the jarred gluten-free marshmallow confection that my kids love. The ideal size for the potatoes is 2 to 4 inches long and ¾ inch wide, or short, fat french fry shapes. I use a french fry cutter and I couldn't recommend it more.

**2½ pounds sweet potatoes, peeled**

**¼ cup canola or olive oil**

**1 teaspoon salt**

**2 teaspoons ground cinnamon**

**Marshmallow Fluff, for serving**

Cut the potatoes with a french fry cutter. To cut by hand, cut long potatoes in half widthwise. Cut the potatoes in equal quarters lengthwise. You will now have 4 long, thick slices for each potato. Turn the slices flat and cut each into 3 or 4 lengthwise strips. You will get 12 to 16 thick fingers from each potato.

Preheat the oven to 425°F.

Transfer the potato fingers to a large bowl. Add the oil, salt, and cinnamon. Toss with a silicone spatula to coat well. Place the potato fingers in a single layer on a parchment paper–lined half sheet pan (18 by 13 inches). Bake until browned and cooked through, about 30 minutes.

Serve with small bowls of Marshmallow Fluff for dipping, or drizzle individual servings with Marshmallow Fluff.

# nachos

• • •

Kids and adults love nachos. They are easy to assemble, they are quick to cook, and variations abound. What makes this recipe special is the portion size: Instead of one huge platter, I make three plates, each serving three people. You can assemble the plates and cook them one at a time, or cook them all at once for a crowd. Use my Chili con Carne (page 132) or a gluten-free prepared version of your choice.

**1 (16-ounce) bag corn tortilla chips**

**3 cups Chili con Carne (page 132) or gluten-free prepared chili of choice, heated**

**1½ cups shredded mild Cheddar cheese or nondairy alternative**

**1½ cups prepared guacamole**

**¾ cup sour cream or nondairy alternative, plus more for garnish**

**¾ cup prepared tomato-based salsa**

**Chopped green onions, for garnish**

**Canned sliced jalapeño peppers, drained, for garnish**

For each 10-inch plate, distribute 36 corn tortilla chips evenly. Top each plate with 1 cup of hot chili, ½ cup of cheese, ½ cup of guacamole, ¼ cup of sour cream, and ¼ cup of salsa. Garnish each plate as desired with a dollop of sour cream in the middle, chopped green onions, and sliced jalapeños.

variation: For a vegetarian version, substitute heated vegetarian refried beans or all-bean chili for the chili con carne.

# quesadillas and beyond

MAKES 1 QUESADILLA

• ● ●

Gluten-free corn tortillas are the foundation for Mexican cheese quesadillas. They can be cooked on the stovetop or in the microwave. The quesadilla idea in our family has been extended to include wide-ranging cheese and ingredient combinations. Beyond quesadillas, we make individual pizzas, breakfast tacos, and even dessert quesadillas. Just follow the recipe here and vary it as you wish.

**2 tablespoons tomato salsa**

**2 (6-inch) corn tortillas**

**¼ cup grated cheese of choice or nondairy alternative**

Spread the salsa on one of the corn tortillas. Sprinkle on the cheese evenly. Top with the second tortilla. Sauté in a nonstick skillet over medium-high heat until the cheese melts. Flip and sauté on the second side.

Alternatively, place the assembled quesadilla on a microwave-safe plate. Weight with a second plate. Microwave until the cheese melts, about 1 minute 30 seconds.

Transfer to a cutting board and cut into 6 wedges.

**variations:** Use only cheese or combinations of cheese between the tortillas.

Use salsa and Monterey Jack or pepper Jack cheese.

Use green tomatillo salsa.

Substitute canned refried beans or White Bean Dip (page 78) for the salsa.

Substitute Hummus (page 75) for the salsa and use grated feta cheese.

Add 2 tablespoons of crumbled crisp bacon, chopped ham, shredded chicken, flaked light tuna, chopped black olives, or flaked smoked salmon to your cheese of choice, such as Cheddar, Swiss, or cream cheese.

Substitute Ten-Minute Barbecue Sauce (page 125) or prepared barbecue sauce for the salsa and cheese, and sprinkle with shredded Barbecue Pulled Pork or Chicken (page 126) or cooked chicken (see page 191).

Substitute peanut butter and jelly for the salsa and cheese.

**FOR A DESSERT QUESADILLA,** substitute cream cheese for the salsa, and thinly sliced ripe banana for the cheese. Sprinkle with chocolate chips. Dust the top of the cooked quesadilla with confectioners' sugar.

**FOR OPEN-FACED PIZZAS,** spread each tortilla with prepared pizza sauce and top with grated mozzarella. Microwave or sauté open faced until the cheese melts.

**FOR BREAKFAST TACOS,** spread each tortilla with cream cheese, sour cream, or a nondairy alternative. Top with a scrambled egg and optional crumbled crisp bacon. Sprinkle with your cheese of choice. Microwave until the cheese melts.

# ham and cheese roll-ups

## MAKES 10 ROLLS

• • •

Sliced ham is a favorite lunch sandwich for many, but when Sarah found she couldn't eat wheat bread, she also found that gluten-free bread was suddenly a scarce commodity and one freshly baked homemade loaf had to last for lunch sandwiches and breakfast toast. So here is a ham and cheese sandwich without the bread.

**1 (8-ounce) package cream cheese, softened, or nondairy alternative**

**½ teaspoon garlic powder**

**½ teaspoon onion powder**

**10 (1-ounce) rectangular or square ham lunch-meat slices**

In a small bowl, combine the cream cheese, garlic powder, and onion powder, and mix well with a silicone spatula.

Place the ham slices on paper towels and pat dry with additional towels.

Spread 1½ tablespoons of cream cheese evenly over 1 slice of the ham, spreading to the edges. Starting at the short end (if using a rectangular slice), roll up tightly and press to seal. Slice diagonally in half. Repeat with the remaining slices.

These can be refrigerated, covered, for up to 4 days, or frozen in layers in an airtight container, separated by parchment paper.

variation: Substitute chicken, turkey, bologna, or another favorite lunch meat for the ham.

# sarah's spring rolls

## MAKES 10 SPRING ROLLS

• • •

Sarah always orders spring rolls at Vietnamese and Thai restaurants, and they are simple to make at home. Spring roll wrappers, available in Asian markets and many supermarkets, can be made both from rice flour (gluten free) and from wheat flour (*not* gluten free), so read the label. To fill these rolls quickly and evenly, divide the ingredients into 10 even piles on top of parchment paper or sheet pans. Then, you'll find that filling and rolling is a snap. I soak 2 wrappers together for easier rolling. You can refrigerate these covered with plastic wrap for up to 3 days, but do not freeze. Serve with bottled Thai sweet red chili sauce, widely available in supermarkets.

**20 peeled, deveined, tail removed, frozen medium shrimp, defrosted**

**Chicken broth**

**½ (10-ounce) bag matchstick carrots**

**4 cups chiffonade of Romaine lettuce (about 1 head) (see Note)**

**¼ cup chiffonade of fresh Thai basil or regular basil**

**⅛ cup chiffonade of fresh mint**

**20 (8-inch) round thin rice flour spring roll wrappers**

**Thai sweet red chili sauce, for dipping**

Place the shrimp in a small saucepan and add chicken broth just to cover. Cook over medium heat just until the shrimp become opaque. Remove from the heat. Let the shrimp marinate in the stock.

Divide all the remaining ingredients except the spring roll wrappers and sauce into 10 equal portions. Lay 10 portions of each ingredient in vertical rows on parchment paper sheets or sheet pans. Drain the shrimp and place 10 portions of 2 shrimp each in a vertical row.

Fill a 12-inch skillet halfway with lukewarm water. Place to the left of a cutting board lined with a paper towel. Place a spring roll wrapper package to the left above the water-filled skillet (so as not to drip water on the dry wrappers). Take 2 wrappers, and soak them together in the water until just pliable, about 30 seconds. Lift with both hands at the top, let drip briefly, and then place the wrappers together on the paper towel. In the middle of the wrapper, place horizontally 1 portion each of carrots, lettuce, shrimp, basil, and mint. Now, as if you were making an envelope starting with its sides, fold the opposite (right-hand and left-hand) sides over the filling as far as they can reach. Fold up the bottom of the spring roll over the sides and over the filling. Then roll tightly over the filling. Place, seam side down, on a parchment paper–lined plate.

Repeat until all the ingredients are used and you have 10 rolls.

Place 1 or 2 spring rolls on each plate. Cut diagonally across the middle. Serve with a bowl of Thai sweet red chili sauce.

note: Chiffonade is a very fine crosswise ribbon cut, thinner than julienne strips, which are vertically cut. To make a chiffonade, slice across the whole lettuce head, or roll up a bunch of lettuce or herb leaves and cut them across the roll.

Chapter 3

# soups, salads, and sandwiches

Chicken Broth and Chicken Meat

Chicken Noodle Soup

Corn and Bacon Chowder

Potato Soup

Creamy Tomato Soup

Ranch-Style Dressing

Dairy-Free Ranch-Style Dressing

Two Vinaigrettes for Green Salad

Egg Salad or Deviled Eggs

Tuna Salad or Tuna Melt

Pasta Salad

Basic Burgers or Meatballs

Grilled Cheese Sandwich

Soups, salads, and sandwiches say "lunch!"; however, the recipes in this chapter could easily serve as first courses or sides for dinner, or as soup-and-sandwich suppers. Every one of the following recipes can be portioned, packed, reheated (when appropriate), and taken to school or friends' houses. Several can be frozen.

Chicken Broth and Chicken Meat (page 91) is an easy but versatile dish: stew, soup, chicken meat, and broth. The other soups are simple to make and lend themselves to a gang of garnishes: popcorn, bacon bits, chopped green onions or parsley, julienned basil, crème fraîche or sour cream, taco chips or potato chips.

The salad dressing recipes—ranch style, mustard vinaigrette, and red French vinaigrette—allow for the possibility of sending a fresh green salad to school for lunch. Pack the dressing in a small plastic container with a tight lid and the salad greens in a 1-quart container with a tight lid and room for tossing. The theory is that the lunch pack is chilled, the dressing can be poured onto the greens, the lid replaced, and the greens tossed by shaking. Frankly, I have had more success packing a salad for dinner at friends' houses than for lunch at school, but perhaps your teen is a salad lover and will welcome a green salad for lunch.

Egg salad doubles as a filling for deviled eggs, and tuna salad can be transformed into a tuna melt. The Pasta Salad (page 101) is absolutely wonderful for a buffet or a crowd, and, no, rice pasta does *not* get mushy in a cold salad if you know the secret preparation trick.

Basic burgers and the Grilled Cheese Sandwich (page 104) are two classic teen favorites, and my favorites, too. Burgers can be frozen and reheated in the microwave, and even the sandwich can be frozen and then reheated until the cheese melts, though the outside will not be as crispy. Grilled cheese sandwiches by another name are panini, and, as with dips, I suggest you dream up your own variations here. It's hard to make a bad grilled cheese combo.

# chicken broth and chicken meat

MAKES 4 QUARTS PLUS 1 CUP BROTH, 6 CUPS SHREDDED CHICKEN

• • •

Prepared chicken broth is a convenient cooking ingredient, but it never tastes quite like the rich homemade broth in Chicken Noodle Soup (page 92). And recipes often call for cooked chicken meat. So here is the best of both worlds: broth and chicken meat. There are two secrets to great flavor: using bouillon cubes instead of salt, and using extra chicken parts. One gluten-free bouillon cube has less than half the sodium in 1 teaspoon of salt. Freeze the defatted broth in quart containers and the shredded chicken meat in 2-cup containers.

1 (4-pound) whole frying chicken

2 pounds wings or bony chicken parts (see Note)

4 carrots, peeled and halved

4 celery ribs, halved

1 medium yellow onion, peeled and halved

3 sprigs fresh thyme, or 1 teaspoon dried

4 peeled garlic cloves

1 bay leaf

4 quarts cold water

4 gluten-free chicken bouillon cubes

Place all the ingredients in an 8- to 10-quart stockpot. Bring to a boil over high heat. Decrease the heat, cover, and let simmer for 1 hour.

Remove the pot from the heat. Strain the broth into a large metal bowl and discard the vegetables, and the giblets and liver, if using, reserving the chicken and wings.

Cool the broth in an ice water bath, then refrigerate, covered, overnight.

Let the chicken cool to room temperature. While the broth is cooling, remove the chicken meat from the bones, including the meaty joints of the wing bones. Discard all the skin and shred the meat with your fingers or 2 forks. Refrigerate until ready to use, or freeze in 2-cup batches.

Remove the congealed surface fat from the refrigerated broth and discard. Transfer the broth to 1-quart containers. Refrigerate until ready to use, or freeze.

note: Supermarkets may not always carry bony chicken parts (necks, backs, wing tips), but they always carry chicken wings. If the whole chicken comes with giblets and the liver, add them to the pot.

suggested use: Make chicken stew by heating 2 quarts of the broth to boiling; add ½ cup each of chopped potatoes, carrots, and celery and ½ cup frozen green peas; and cook until tender. Stir in 3 cups of the chicken meat and heat through.

# chicken noodle soup

## MAKES 8 SERVINGS

• ● •

I usually use homemade chicken broth (see page 91) for this soup, but when there's none in the freezer and I'm crunched for time, I use prepared broth. The vegetables, noodles, and chicken meat make a hearty dish.

**2 quarts chicken broth, homemade (see page 91) or prepared**

**2 cups crosswise-sliced peeled carrots**

**1 cup finely diced yellow onions**

**1 cup thinly sliced celery**

**1 cup frozen green peas**

**4 ounces short brown rice pasta (fusilli, penne, shells, or spirals) (preferably Tinkyáda)**

**2 cups shredded cooked chicken (see page 91)**

In a 4-quart pot, bring the broth to a boil over high heat. Add all the other ingredients except for the chicken. Bring to a boil, stirring. Decrease the heat immediately, cover, and simmer until the pasta is cooked, 15 to 20 minutes.

Uncover, add the chicken, and stir. Cook until heated through, about 5 more minutes. Ladle into soup bowls.

**variations:** Substitute ¼ to ½ cup white long-grain rice for the pasta.

Substitute 1 cup cubed peeled red-skinned potatoes for the pasta.

For a more stew-like dish, increase the pasta to 8 ounces.

Garnish with crisp taco strips, chopped flat-leaf parsley, or green onions.

# corn and bacon chowder

MAKES 8 CUPS, 6 TO 8 SERVINGS

• • •

Chowders have been American favorites with people of all ages since the 1700s. The flavor of this simple soup depends completely on the quality of the corn—fresh, frozen, or canned. The better the flavor, the better the soup. I make this in the summer using farmers' market fresh corn, but in the winter, I use top-quality frozen or premium canned corn.

**8 slices bacon, finely chopped**

**3 cups chopped peeled russet potatoes**

**3 cups corn kernels (freshly cut from the cobs, or defrosted frozen, or drained canned)**

**1 quart chicken broth (see page 91)**

**½ teaspoon salt**

**Popcorn, for garnish**

**Green onions, thinly sliced crosswise, for garnish**

**Chopped flat-leaf parsley, for garnish**

In a 3-quart saucepan over medium heat, fry the bacon, stirring, until crisp. Remove from the pan and drain on paper towels. Pour the bacon fat from the pan, and return 1 tablespoon to the pan. Add the potatoes and stir. Add the corn and stir. Add the chicken broth and salt, increase the heat, and bring to a boil, stirring. Decrease the heat, cover, and simmer for 30 minutes.

Puree the vegetables coarsely in the pan using an immersion blender, or let the soup cool and transfer in batches to a blender or food processor. Do not puree too smoothly.

Serve garnished with the bacon bits and, if desired, popcorn, green onions, or parsley.

# potato soup

MAKES 8 TO 10 SERVINGS

● ● ●

Potato soup is good hot or cold—cold in hot weather and hot in cold weather. My kids will eat it cold in the summer if I serve it with a Grilled Cheese Sandwich (page 104) on the side. The rest of the year, I serve it hot. It can start the meal or even be the meal (lunch or supper) served with an All-Day Breakfast Sandwich (page 71), a burger (see page 103), or an egg salad sandwich (see page 99). Try garnishing it with popcorn, bacon bits, or chopped green onion, or serve it with a side of potato chips.

**3 tablespoons canola oil**

**2 cups diced leeks, white and pale green parts only**

**2 quarts chicken broth**

**4 cups diced peeled russet potatoes**

**¾ cup half-and-half**

**½ teaspoon salt, or to taste**

In an 8-quart pot over medium heat, heat the oil. Add the leeks and cook, stirring, until they are tender, but not browned, 5 to 6 minutes. Add the chicken broth and the potatoes and bring to a boil. Decrease the heat and simmer until the potatoes are cooked and tender, 30 to 35 minutes, stirring often from the bottom to prevent burning.

Puree with an immersion blender. Or let the soup cool and puree in batches in a blender or food processor. Return the pureed soup to the pot and heat over medium heat, stirring. Add the half-and-half and let simmer for 5 minutes. Season to taste with salt.

variations: **Substitute vegetable broth for the chicken broth.**

**Substitute Yukon gold potatoes for the russet potatoes.**

# creamy tomato soup

### MAKES 6 CUPS, 6 SERVINGS

• • •

Better tasting and less expensive than the canned version, this tomato soup is easy and uncomplicated. Serve it plain for kids, or garnished with popcorn, and for adults or more adventuresome teens, garnish it with diced tomato and chiffonade of fresh basil.

**2 tablespoons canola or extra virgin olive oil**

**½ cup diced onion**

**½ cup diced celery**

**1 teaspoon minced garlic**

**2 tablespoons Gluten-Free All-Purpose Flour (page 43) or flour of choice with xanthan gum in the mix**

**1 quart tomato juice**

**2 cups chicken broth**

**3 tablespoons tomato paste**

**1 cup heavy cream**

**Salt to taste**

**Popcorn, for garnish**

**1 cup diced seeded tomato (optional)**

**1 tablespoon chiffonade of fresh basil (see Note, page 86; optional)**

In a heavy 4-quart saucepan over medium heat, heat the oil. Add the onion, celery, and garlic and sauté for 4 minutes. Add the flour and cook for 2 minutes, stirring often.

Add the tomato juice, chicken broth, and tomato paste; stir well, and bring to a boil. Decrease the heat and simmer for 20 to 25 minutes. Puree the soup using an immersion blender. Or let cool and transfer in batches to a blender or food processor and puree, then return to the pot.

Stir in the heavy cream and simmer for 5 more minutes. Season with salt, if needed.

Serve hot or cold. Ladle the soup into individual bowls, garnishing with popcorn, tomato, or basil.

variation: For nondairy soup, substitute nondairy sour cream for the cream.

# ranch-style dressing

• • •

Ranch-style dressing is my kids' favorite. And, yes, I can buy several prepared brands, some gluten free. But after reading the ingredients labels, I decided I could create a more natural, completely chemical-free, less expensive version.

½ cup mayonnaise (not made with grapeseed or strong-tasting oil)

½ cup buttermilk

½ cup sour cream

1½ teaspoons sugar

1 teaspoon onion powder

½ teaspoon garlic powder

½ teaspoon dried parsley

½ teaspoon salt

Place all the ingredients in a 1-quart bowl and whisk to mix well. Transfer to a glass or plastic container. Cover and refrigerate for at least 4 hours before using. The dressing will keep for up to 7 days covered and refrigerated.

# dairy-free ranch-style dressing

MAKES ABOUT 1½ CUPS

• • •

Sarah is lactose intolerant, so this recipe is for her and for kids like her who don't tolerate dairy well. Mayonnaise contains no dairy products.

½ cup mayonnaise (not made with grapeseed or strong-tasting oil) or mayonnaise alternative (preferably Vegenaise)

¾ cup nondairy sour cream

¼ cup nondairy beverage (rice or soy)

2 teaspoons sugar

1½ teaspoons rice vinegar

1 teaspoon onion powder

½ teaspoon garlic powder

½ teaspoon dried parsley

½ teaspoon salt

Place all the ingredients in a 1-quart bowl and whisk well to mix. Transfer to a plastic or glass container and refrigerate, covered, for at least 4 hours before using. The dressing will keep for up to 7 days covered and refrigerated.

# two vinaigrettes for green salad

• • •

Many kids don't like "bits" in their food; appreciation for texture often comes with age. My kids and their friends will eat green salad if the dressing is smooth, tasty, and not too sour. Here are two of their favorites. Each makes ⅓ cup, enough to dress 6 to 8 cups of salad greens. When measuring honey, it may help to spray the teaspoon lightly with nonstick cooking spray first, so all the honey will slide right off. For extra creamy emulsified dressing, add 1 teaspoon of mayonnaise to either of these options before whisking.

## honey-mustard vinaigrette

• • •

**2 tablespoons rice vinegar**

**2 tablespoons olive oil**

**2 teaspoons honey**

**1 teaspoon Dijon mustard**

**½ teaspoon salt**

Measure all the ingredients in the order given into a small bowl or a measuring cup with a spout. Whisk until the salt is dissolved and the dressing is emulsified.

Use right away or transfer to a plastic or glass container and refrigerate, covered. Whisk again before using. The dressing will keep for up to 7 days covered and refrigerated.

variation: Add ½ teaspoon pureed garlic, which is available in a tube or jar. To puree your own, smash a peeled garlic clove with the side of a knife, then chop finely until pureed.

## red french vinaigrette

• • •

**2 tablespoons rice vinegar**

**2 tablespoons ketchup**

**2 tablespoons canola oil**

**1 teaspoon honey**

**½ teaspoon garlic powder**

**½ teaspoon onion powder**

**½ teaspoon salt**

Measure all the ingredients in the order given into a small bowl or a measuring cup with a spout. Whisk until the salt is dissolved and the dressing is emulsified.

Use right away or transfer to a plastic or glass container and refrigerate, covered. Whisk again before using. The dressing will keep for up to 7 days covered and refrigerated.

# egg salad or deviled eggs

## MAKES 4 CUPS

● ● ●

Everyone has their own egg salad recipe, and mine was a family favorite that remained unchanged until Sarah became intolerant of a lot of dairy foods. So I changed the recipe with a nondairy alternative. Both versions taste equally good. An egg slicer becomes a perfect egg chopper, as you will see. And cabbage is an excellent stand-in for celery. While it's great on White Sandwich Bread (page 45), it is also good scooped onto lettuce and served as a salad, garnished with tomatoes. And don't forget deviled eggs (see Variations).

**12 hard-boiled eggs, peeled**

**1 cup finely diced celery, or finely shredded cabbage, chopped**

**½ cup minced onion**

**½ cup mayonnaise or gluten-free dressing of choice**

**3 tablespoons sour cream or nondairy alternative**

**1 tablespoon Dijon mustard**

**1 teaspoon finely grated lemon zest**

**½ teaspoon salt**

Slice each egg lengthwise in a wire egg slicer. Then reverse the egg and slice horizontally. Alternatively, chop the eggs finely with a knife.

Place the chopped eggs and all the other ingredients in a medium bowl and mix well with a silicone spatula. Cover and refrigerate for at least 4 hours or overnight.

variations: Add lettuce or ham to your egg salad sandwich.

TO MAKE DEVILED EGGS: Halve the eggs and reserve the whites. Chop and mix the yolks with the remaining recipe ingredients until creamy. Use the mixture to fill the reserved whites. Cover and refrigerate.

# tuna salad or tuna melt

### MAKES ABOUT 2 CUPS

• • •

Tuna salad on crisp lettuce is a summer favorite, and tuna sandwiches made with White Sandwich Bread (page 45) are popular all year round, as are tuna melts (see Variation). Canned light tuna in several brands, including Chicken of the Sea and Bumble Bee, is gluten free, but always check the brand online, as products change. "Light" doesn't mean low fat; it means light meat as opposed to white meat. Light tuna has less mercury than white as well. One day, I ran out of celery and substituted prepared cole slaw mix. Nobody knew the difference. The flavor was excellent and the cabbage held up as well as celery.

**3 (5-ounce) cans light tuna in water, drained**

**½ cup minced celery, or finely shredded cabbage, chopped**

**¼ cup minced yellow onion**

**1 teaspoon finely grated lemon zest**

**1 teaspoon Dijon mustard**

**¾ cup mayonnaise, or to taste**

In a medium bowl, mix together all the ingredients except the mayonnaise. Then add the mayonnaise and mix well. Cover and refrigerate. Stir before using.

**variation:** To make a tuna melt: Place a 1-ounce slice of cheese of choice or nondairy alternative on top of the tuna salad on a slice of bread, but do not top with a second piece of bread. Bake at 400°F until the cheese melts.

# pasta salad

## MAKES 8 TO 10 SERVINGS

• • •

There is one secret to great gluten-free pasta salads: Keep your ingredients dry. This pasta salad can be refrigerated for 4 days without getting mushy, the protein ingredients can be widely varied, and you can make nondairy and vegetarian versions. Frozen peas and carrots are convenient and have already been blanched. Use short pasta such as fusilli, penne, shells, or spirals.

**1 pound short brown rice pasta, preferably Tinkyáda, cooked, drained, and rinsed**

**1 cup frozen green peas, thawed**

**¼ cup shredded carrot**

**1 (15-ounce) can black beans, rinsed and drained**

**1½ cups mayonnaise**

**½ cup sour cream or nondairy alternative**

**2 tablespoons rice wine vinegar**

**1 teaspoon garlic powder**

**1 teaspoon onion powder**

**½ teaspoon salt**

**2 cups Barbecue Pulled Pork or Chicken (page 126), or shredded cooked chicken (see page 91), or diced ham**

**1 cup frozen corn, thawed**

**½ cup finely diced celery**

**¼ cup finely diced yellow onion**

Spread the cooked pasta on a parchment paper–lined half sheet pan (18 by 13 inches) to cool and dry. Let rest for 20 minutes.

Spread the peas, carrot, and beans on a tray lined with 3 thicknesses of paper towels to dry. Let rest for 20 minutes.

Meanwhile, make the dressing: Place the mayonnaise, sour cream, vinegar, garlic powder, onion powder, and salt in a small bowl and whisk well to mix.

In a 6-quart bowl, place the pasta, pork or chicken or ham, peas, carrot, beans, corn, celery, and onion. Add the dressing and toss gently but thoroughly with a silicone spatula. Cover and refrigerate for at least 4 hours or overnight. Toss before serving.

**variations:** **FOR A VEGETARIAN VERSION,** omit the meat and substitute 1 cup of diced mild Cheddar or a cheese of your choice.

Substitute 4 (5-ounce) cans of well-drained light tuna for the meat.

# basic burgers or meatballs

## MAKES 4 LARGE BURGERS OR 24 (2-INCH) MEATBALLS

• • •

My basic burger can be made with ground beef, turkey, or chicken. The seasoning is savory but mild, and picky eaters who balk at "bits" in food won't have a clue that the mixture contains healthful vegetables. Use this recipe for burgers, meatballs, and breakfast sausage. Cooked burgers may be wrapped and frozen for reheating in the microwave. The uncooked burger mixture can be frozen (as long as the meat was not previously frozen) in an airtight lidded container and defrosted and cooked at a later date. Don't forget to label and date it. It will keep for up to 1 month. To grill on an outdoor grill, add 1 egg and mix well. Then form into patties.

½ cup coarsely chopped onion

1 celery rib, coarsely chopped

1 medium carrot, coarsely chopped

2 tablespoons canola or extra virgin olive oil

1 pound lean ground beef, turkey, or chicken

½ cup crushed gluten-free crackers, or ⅓ cup gluten-free bread crumbs

1 teaspoon salt

White Sandwich Bread (page 45) or Hamburger Buns (page 49), for serving

Toppings and condiments of choice, for serving

In the work bowl of a food processor fitted with the metal blade, combine the onion, celery, and carrot. Pulse and process to mince finely, scraping down the sides of the bowl as necessary. Add the oil and process to puree. Add the meat, crackers or bread crumbs, and salt, and pulse to mix well. At this point, the burger mixture can be tightly wrapped and refrigerated for up to 3 days.

Divide the meat into 4 equal portions. Wet your hands with cold water and shape 5-inch diameter patties; pat down to level. Spray a 12-inch nonstick skillet with nonstick cooking spray, heat to medium-high, and fry the burgers until browned on one side, 5 to 6 minutes; then turn and fry until cooked through, an additional 5 to 6 minutes.

Serve on gluten-free bread or hamburger buns with your choice of toppings and condiments.

variations: TO MAKE MEATBALLS, scoop a level 2-tablepoon measure (⅛ cup) of the burger mixture. With wet hands, form into balls and place on a parchment paper–lined half sheet pan (18 by 13 inches). Spray the meatballs lightly with nonstick cooking spray and bake in a 400°F oven until cooked through, 20 to 25 minutes.

TO MAKE ITALIAN MEATBALLS, add 2 teaspoons garlic powder, 2 teaspoons onion powder, 2 teaspoons dried parsley, and ½ to ¾ cup finely grated Parmesan cheese.

# grilled cheese sandwich

## MAKES 6 SANDWICHES

• ● •

White Sandwich Bread (page 45) makes great grilled cheese sandwiches with endless variations. You can also use your favorite prepared gluten-free bread. Serve the sandwich with Crispy Oven French Fries (page 139) and Cole Slaw (page 137) for lunch or supper all year round.

**12 slices White Sandwich Bread (page 45) or gluten-free bread of choice**

**12 (1-ounce) slices aged Cheddar or Gruyère cheese or nondairy alternative**

**Melted butter or nondairy alternative, for brushing**

Lay 6 slices of the bread on a clean surface and top each with 2 slices of the cheese. Close the sandwiches with the remaining 6 slices of bread. Brush both sides of each sandwich lightly with butter.

Cook each sandwich in a sandwich press or in a nonstick skillet. If using a skillet, weight each sandwich with an 8-inch cake pan holding a 28-ounce can. Cook the first side until golden brown. Remove the weight, flip the sandwich, and cook on the second side until golden brown and the cheese melts.

Slice each sandwich in half to serve.

**variations:** Substitute Berghoff Tastes-Like-Rye Bread (page 50) for the White Sandwich Bread (page 45).

Brush 1 slice of the bread with Dijon mustard before assembling and cooking each sandwich.

Add paper-thin tomato slices to each sandwich before closing and cooking.

Add paper-thin apple and ham slices to each sandwich before closing and cooking.

Add 2 halved crisp-cooked bacon slices to each sandwich before closing and cooking.

Chapter 4

# main dishes

Basic Tomato Sauce

Spaghetti and Meatballs

Linguine Alfredo-Style

Spaghetti Pie

Pizza

Lasagna

Macaroni and Cheese

Crispy Fish or Chicken

Chicken, Broccoli, and Carrot Stir-Fry

Lemon Chicken

Ten-Minute Barbecue Sauce

Barbecue Pulled Pork or Chicken

Barbecue Baby Back Ribs

Meat-and-Vegetable Stew du Jour

Taco Pie

Chili con Carne

Shrimp Fried Rice

Main dishes in our house mean dinner, but we also serve them on buffets and at parties. All of the main dish recipes in this chapter can be frozen (in the case of pasta with sauce, just the sauce) and reheated in the microwave or oven, which also makes them ideal for school lunch leftovers the next day.

Teens are more adventuresome eaters than young children, and teens almost universally like Italian, Mexican, Asian, and regional American foods. So, no surprise here, the recipes in this chapter fall into those four categories, and several of them were high on the list of survey teens' thirty foods they missed the most.

Italian entrees include the Basic Tomato Sauce (page 109)—one of the easiest, sweetest sauces I have ever made. Several other recipes use it, including Spaghetti and Meatballs (page 110), Spaghetti Pie (page 112), and Lasagna (page 116). Of course, we have a pizza recipe, too.

Mexican dishes include the familiar Chili con Carne (page 132) and a less familiar version of *chilaquiles*, taco pie. The Taco Pie (page 131) is made on the stovetop, so it's a quick, savory one-dish meal.

One of the Asian dishes, Chicken, Broccoli, and Carrot Stir-Fry (page 122), is meant to be served with white rice. When I prepare it, I always cook extra rice and refrigerate it for Shrimp Fried Rice (page 133).

Two of the six American dishes depend on one recipe, Ten-Minute Barbecue Sauce (page 125). Use it with Barbecue Pulled Pork or Chicken (page 126) and Barbecue Baby Back Ribs (page 128) for rich, satisfying flavors and completely gluten-free barbecue. What would my kids do without Macaroni and Cheese (page 118)? Here it's made with a cheese sauce that doubles as a vegetable sauce. The Meat-and-Vegetable Stew du Jour (page 129) is a great way to take advantage of meat specials at the market—chicken, turkey, beef, or pork. And I have also satisfied my children's appetite for crisp deep-fried fish and chicken fingers with Crispy Fish or Chicken (page 120), with a surprising and completely successful breading. Try it. You'll like it.

# basic tomato sauce

• • •

This savory, multipurpose tomato sauce may be used to sauce pasta, to make Lasagna (page 116), as the base for a dipping sauce, as the base for Chili con Carne (page 132), and more. It is quick and easy because all the work of chopping up the usual vegetables—celery, carrot, onion, and garlic—is done in the food processor.

**1 cup coarsely chopped yellow onions**

**1 celery rib, coarsely chopped**

**1 medium carrot, coarsely chopped**

**1 garlic clove**

**2 tablespoons extra virgin olive oil**

**1 (29-ounce) can tomato puree or crushed tomatoes**

**½ cup water**

**1 teaspoon salt**

In the work bowl of a large-capacity food processor (12 to 14 cups) fitted with the steel blade, combine the onions, celery, carrot, and garlic. Pulse to chop very finely, scraping down the sides of the bowl as necessary. Add the oil. Process to puree the vegetables. Add the tomato puree, water, and salt. Process until smooth, about 2 minutes.

Transfer the contents to a 3-quart saucepan. Bring to a boil over high heat, stirring constantly. Decrease the heat (or if your stove is electric, move the pan to another burner), cover, and simmer steadily, stirring occasionally to prevent burning, for 30 minutes.

variations: **FOR ITALIAN TOMATO SAUCE,** add 1 teaspoon of dried oregano and 1 teaspoon of dried basil to the sauce and simmer to meld the flavors. Or simply add 2 teaspoons of Italian seasoning blend. Increase the seasoning to suit your taste.

# spaghetti and meatballs

## MAKES 6 TO 8 SERVINGS

• • •

This is a favorite family dinner, and because there are good gluten-free pastas available, nobody misses wheat pasta. Leftovers can be refrigerated and reheated in the microwave and small portions make an excellent school lunch or portable dinner for a school event.

**1 recipe Basic Tomato Sauce, Italian variation (page 109), or 4 cups jarred pasta sauce**

**1 recipe Italian meatballs (see page 103), cooked**

**Salt**

**1 pound brown rice spaghetti or linguine**

**Finely grated Parmesan cheese, for serving**

In a 6-quart pot over medium heat, cook the tomato sauce until hot, stirring occasionally. Add the cooked meatballs and cook for 20 minutes, stirring gently and frequently to prevent the bottom of the pot from burning.

Meanwhile, in an 8-quart pot, bring 6 quarts of water to a boil. Add 1 tablespoon of salt. Add the spaghetti or linguine (preferably Tinkyáda), or pasta shape of your choice (such as penne or fusilli), and cook according to the package directions. Drain.

Return the pasta to the pot. Add the sauce and meatballs and toss gently with a silicone spatula to coat. Serve in bowls, accompanied by a bowl of Parmesan cheese.

# linguine alfredo-style

• • •

Authentic Alfredo sauce depends on heavy cream, butter, and Parmesan cheese—not a low-calorie dish. One cup (8 ounces) of butter has 1,600 calories. This sauce has less than half the calories, because it uses cream cheese (800 calories) instead of butter, and milk instead of cream. It is an occasional treat that my kids enjoy.

**2 cups whole milk (regular or lactose free)**

**8 ounces cream cheese, cut into 8 squares, or nondairy alternative**

**1 cup finely grated Parmesan cheese**

**1 teaspoon garlic powder**

**½ teaspoon salt**

**1 pound cooked brown rice linguine or spaghetti**

In a 2-quart saucepan over medium heat, cook the milk, stirring, until hot. Add the cream cheese and cook, whisking, until the cheese is completely melted and the sauce is smooth. Add the Parmesan, garlic powder, and salt, and cook, whisking constantly, until the sauce is smooth and thick.

Pour the sauce over the hot cooked pasta in a large bowl and toss to mix completely. Serve in individual bowls.

# spaghetti pie

MAKES 8 TO 12 SERVINGS

● ● ●

This casserole delivers all the savory goodness of lasagna—meat, cheese, sauce, and noodles—but is easier to prepare. Be sure to cook the rice spaghetti according to the package directions. Drain it, rinse it under cold running water, and drain it well once more before layering it in the casserole. For a nondairy version, use nondairy cheeses.

**1 pound ground turkey**

**1 teaspoon garlic powder**

**1 teaspoon onion powder**

**1 teaspoon dried oregano**

**1 teaspoon salt**

**4 cups Basic Tomato Sauce (page 109) or jarred pasta sauce**

**1 pound dry rice spaghetti (preferably Tinkyáda), cooked and drained**

**3 cups (12 ounces) grated mozzarella cheese, Soyrella, or casein-free nondairy alternative**

**½ cup (2 ounces) finely grated aged Parmesan cheese or nondairy alternative**

Spray a 12-inch sauté pan with nonstick cooking spray and heat over medium heat. Place the turkey in the pan and sprinkle with the garlic powder, onion powder, oregano, and salt. Cook, breaking up the meat into small pieces with a spatula, until browned, about 15 minutes. Remove from the heat and reserve.

Preheat the oven to 375°F. Spray a 9 by 13 by 2-inch glass baking pan with nonstick cooking spray. Ladle ½ cup of the tomato sauce into the bottom, tilting the casserole to cover. Spread one-third of the cooked spaghetti over the sauce. Top with one-half of the turkey and 1 cup of the mozzarella. Top evenly with 2 cups of the sauce. Repeat with one-third of the spaghetti, the remaining turkey, and 1 cup of the mozzarella. Top evenly with 1 cup of the sauce. Repeat with the remaining spaghetti, remaining ½ cup of sauce, and remaining 1 cup of the mozzarella. Sprinkle evenly with the Parmesan cheese.

Spray a 12 by 14-inch piece of foil with nonstick cooking spray. Cover the casserole with the foil, sprayed side down. Place in the oven and bake for 30 minutes. Remove the foil; return the casserole to the oven and bake, uncovered, until browned, an additional 15 minutes.

Remove from the oven and let rest for 15 minutes. Cut the casserole 2 by 4 into 8 pieces, or 3 by 4 into 12 pieces.

# pizza

MAKES ONE 12-INCH ROUND PIZZA

• • •

Pizza ranks in the top ten foods that kids surveyed missed most. Pizza toppings are no problem; most can easily be gluten free. It's the crust that counts. This recipe has a tender texture strong enough to support a load of sauce, cheese, and meat, and a flavor good enough to be very lightly topped. A simple technique for stretching the dough in the pan makes preparation easy. The partially baked crust can be allowed to cool and then be wrapped and frozen. The dough can be frozen in a self-sealing plastic bag sprayed inside with nonstick cooking spray. Top the crust with pizza sauce and your favorite toppings.

## pizza sauce

1 (6-ounce) can tomato paste

1 cup water

1 tablespoon honey

1 teaspoon dried oregano

## pizza crust

1½ cups Gluten-Free All-Purpose Flour (page 43) or flour of choice with xanthan gum in the mix

2 tablespoons nonfat dry milk powder

2 tablespoons finely grated Parmesan cheese

1 tablespoon sugar

1 tablespoon dried egg whites

1½ teaspoons bread machine or instant yeast

1 teaspoon baking powder

½ teaspoon salt

1 cup warm (about 110°F) water

3 tablespoons extra virgin olive oil

1½ to 2 cups shredded mozzarella, Soyrella, or casein-free nondairy alternative

Toppings of choice

**To make the pizza sauce:** In a small bowl, whisk together the tomato paste, water, honey, and oregano until smooth. Refrigerate, covered, until ready to use.

**To make the pizza crust:** Place the flour, milk powder, Parmesan cheese, sugar, dried egg whites, yeast, baking powder, and salt in the work bowl of a stand mixer fitted with the flat beater attachment. Mix on low. Alternatively, place the dry ingredients in a large bowl and mix on low with a sturdy handheld mixer. Add the water and olive oil and mix on low until a dough forms, scraping down the sides of the bowl as necessary. Increase the speed and beat for 5 minutes.

With the beater paddle still attached, cover the bowl with plastic wrap and let the dough rise for 1 hour. If using a handheld mixer, remove and scrape down the beater blades, cover the bowl with plastic wrap, and let the dough rise for about

1 hour or until doubled in size. Mix on low to deflate.

Spray a 12-inch round pizza pan well with nonstick cooking spray. Using a silicone spatula, scrape the dough onto the pan. Spray the palms of both your hands with nonstick cooking spray, or oil your palms by rubbing them on a plate containing 2 tablespoons of cooking oil. Using your hands, press the dough outward to fill the edges of the pan, smoothing the dough as level as possible. Let the dough rise in the pan in a warm place for 15 to 20 minutes.

Preheat the oven to 425°F.

Bake the dough for 10 minutes. Remove from the oven. For each 12-inch round pizza crust, use ¼ cup of the pizza sauce to spread over the top. Sprinkle with the cheese or nondairy alternative and other toppings of choice. Return the pizza to the oven and bake until the crust is browned around the rim, the cheese is bubbling, and the pizza is heated through, about 15 minutes. Let rest for 5 to 10 minutes. Then slide out of the pan with a spatula and cut into 8 wedges.

**variations:** Add 1 cup of sautéed bulk Italian sausage or 12 thin slices of pepperoni to the top of the cheese.

# lasagna

## MAKES 8 TO 10 SERVINGS

• • •

Lasagna would be my choice for the most versatile dish: Once assembled, it cooks unattended. It stays warm and holds well. It freezes and travels well. It makes a great buffet or party dish, or family dinner. Leftovers can be reheated. And now that there are excellent gluten-free brown rice lasagna noodles, it can be so tasty, nobody will know it was not made with traditional wheat pasta. You will need 2 (10-ounce) packages for 12 noodles and will have some noodles left over. Use oven-ready, no-boiling noodles to avoid having to precook the noodles.

**2 tablespoons extra virgin olive oil**

**1 recipe basic burger meat, Italian seasoning variation (see page 103)**

**1 recipe Basic Tomato Sauce, Italian variation (page 109)**

**12 long oven-ready, no-boiling brown rice lasagna noodles (preferably DeBoles)**

**1 pound shredded mozzarella or scamorze cheese**

**1 cup finely grated aged Parmesan cheese**

Preheat the oven to 375°F. Spray a 9 by 13 by 2-inch glass baking pan with nonstick cooking spray.

Heat the oil in a 12-inch nonstick skillet over medium heat. Add the meat, increase the heat to medium-high, and sauté, stirring to break up the clumps, until the meat is browned. Remove the skillet from the heat and reserve.

Place 1 cup of the sauce in the baking pan and tilt to cover the bottom. Lay 4 uncooked lasagna noodles side by side, slightly overlapping. Cover evenly with 1 cup of the sauce, one-half of the sautéed meat, one-third of the mozzarella, and ⅓ cup of the Parmesan cheese. Top with 4 more noodles. Cover the noodles with 1 cup of the sauce,

the remaining half of the meat, another third of the mozzarella, and ⅓ cup of the Parmesan. Top with the remaining 4 noodles and cover evenly (be sure to cover the edges) with the remaining 1 cup of sauce. Spray a 9 by 14-inch length of foil with nonstick cooking spray. Place, sprayed side down, on the baking dish and crimp to cover.

Bake, covered, for 1 hour. Remove the foil and sprinkle evenly with the remaining one-third mozzarella and ⅓ cup of Parmesan. Bake, uncovered, until the top is browned, about 15 minutes.

Remove from the oven. Let cool for 15 minutes. Cut 2 by 4 for 8 pieces, or 3 by 4 for 12 pieces.

**notes:** To make the lasagna easier to handle in the oven, place the baking dish on a half sheet pan (18 by 13 inches).

Lasagna will keep, covered, in the refrigerator for up to 4 days and can be reheated in the microwave. You can freeze individual portions in lidded containers. Defrost before reheating in the microwave.

**variations:** Substitute 4 cups of canned tomato puree or crushed tomatoes mixed with 1 tablespoon Italian seasoning for the tomato sauce.

Substitute 1 pound of ground beef, turkey, or chicken sprinkled with ½ teaspoon of salt and sautéed for the Italian-seasoned basic burger meat.

Substitute 1 pound of sweet Italian sausage (preferably Jennie-O or Johnsonville) for the basic burger meat; omit the oil and brown the sausage in a nonstick skillet.

**FOR A LACTOSE-FREE VERSION,** substitute aged Gruyère or casein-free nondairy mozzarella for the mozzarella in the recipe.

# macaroni and cheese

## MAKES 8 SIDE-DISH OR 4 TO 6 MAIN-DISH SERVINGS

• • •

Kids are familiar with the quick and easy macaroni and cheese boxed mix, and there are some gluten-free versions, but the serving size is small and the price seems high to me. This recipe uses a gluten-free version of classic French Mornay sauce (cream sauce with cheese added). I have added more cheese and stepped up the flavor with garlic, mustard, and onion powders. It freezes well, and leftover sauce is great on vegetables. Be sure to use aged cheeses, which melt well, for the lactose intolerant. I always grate my own cheese in the food processor (see Notes), but pre-grated cheese still works; just make sure it's gluten free, and stir it well.

**1 pound short brown rice pasta (preferably Tinkyáda), such as macaroni, fusilli, penne, or spirals**

**2 to 3 cups warm Cheese Sauce (recipe follows)**

Cook the pasta according to the package directions. Remove and reserve 1 cup of the pasta cooking water. Drain the pasta, but do not rinse. Return the pasta to the cooking pot. Stir in the cheese sauce (start with 2 cups), tossing gently with a silicone spatula to coat the pasta. If the mixture is too thick, add the reserved pasta water by the ¼ cup and mix well. Serve warm.

# cheese sauce

## MAKES 6 TO 7 CUPS

• • •

¼ cup (½ stick) butter or nondairy alternative

½ cup Gluten-Free All-Purpose Flour (page 43) or flour of choice with xanthan gum in the mix

1 teaspoon garlic powder

1 teaspoon mustard powder

1 teaspoon onion powder

1 teaspoon salt

4 cups whole milk (regular or lactose free) or nondairy alternative (rice or soy)

2 cups (8 ounces) grated aged Cheddar or Gruyère cheese

In a 3-quart saucepan over medium heat, melt the butter.

In a small bowl, mix together the flour, garlic powder, mustard powder, onion powder, and salt. Add to the melted butter and whisk to a smooth paste. Cook for 2 minutes, whisking. Remove the pan from the heat. Pour in the milk all at once. Whisk until the sauce is smooth.

Return the pan to the heat and whisk constantly until the sauce thickens and comes to a full boil, 8 to 10 minutes. Remove from the heat. Stir in the cheese in 3 batches, whisking constantly until the cheese melts and the sauce is smooth.

notes: Pre-grated packaged cheese is a great convenience but is usually coated with a starch to prevent clumping and rarely melts as well as freshly grated cheese. To grate cheese quickly, cut it into 1-inch chunks and pulse to peppercorn-sized pieces in a food processor fitted with the steel blade.

You can store unused sauce: Let the sauce cool to room temperature and refrigerate, covered, for up to 4 days. The sauce can also be frozen. Defrost over simmering water before reheating.

variation: Substitute nondairy cheese for dairy cheese.

# crispy fish or chicken

## MAKES 6 SERVINGS

• • •

According to our survey, kids sorely missed crispy breaded and fried fish and chicken strips. Prepared ready-made gluten-free breading fell short of my family's expectations. This recipe, however, got rave reviews. The secret is using gluten-free crispy brown rice cereal (generic or brand name) for the breading, and adding flavor to the beaten eggs. The fish or chicken may be served as a snack or a main dish. Brining before cooking makes the fish and chicken sweet and moist, but this step is optional. This is great with a side of Cole Slaw (page 137).

**6 tilapia fillets (about 1½ pounds), or 1½ pounds chicken tenders**

**2 cups rice milk (or to cover; optional)**

**1 teaspoon salt (optional)**

**2 eggs well beaten with 2 tablespoons water**

**1 tablespoon Dijon mustard**

**3 cups gluten-free crispy brown rice cereal**

**Prepared gluten-free tartar sauce or Ten-Minute Barbecue Sauce (page 125), as needed for serving**

Cut the tilapia fillets in half lengthwise. If using chicken tenders, pull out the white tendons and discard. Place the fish or chicken in a glass baking pan. In a small bowl, mix the rice milk and salt, if desired, and stir to dissolve the salt. Pour over the fish or chicken and let rest for 30 minutes, or cover and refrigerate for several hours or overnight.

Remove the fish or chicken from the rice milk brine and pat dry with paper towels.

Preheat the oven to 400°F. Line a half sheet pan (18 by 13 inches) with parchment paper, and spray with nonstick cooking spray.

In a small bowl, mix the egg-water mixture with the mustard; whisk to mix well. Pour into a shallow bowl.

Place the brown rice cereal in a 1-gallon self-sealing plastic bag, squeeze out the air, and seal. Using a rolling pin, roll to crush the cereal to fine crumbs, leaving some coarse pieces intact. Transfer the crushed cereal to a large flat plate.

One by one, dip the fish fillet halves or chicken tenders first in the egg-mustard mixture, turning to coat each side well, then in the cereal, turning and patting to coat well. Transfer to the parchment paper–lined pan. Spray the tops of the fish or chicken lightly with nonstick cooking spray and bake until cooked through and crisp, 30 to 35 minutes.

Remove the pan from the oven and transfer the fish or chicken to a serving platter. Serve with tartar sauce or Ten-Minute Barbecue Sauce (page 125).

**variation:** For crispy chicken thighs, substitute 6 boneless, skinless chicken thighs for the fish fillets. Trim the thighs of excess fat and cut in half before coating. Increase the oven temperature to 425°F and bake for 35 minutes.

# chicken, broccoli, and carrot stir-fry

### MAKES 6 SERVINGS

• • •

Asian restaurants often have a lot of good gluten-free options. At home, my family likes this homemade version of a stir-fry with lots of sauce served over cooked white rice. Try to cut the broccoli into small, equal florets, so they cook uniformly. The seasoning sauce added at the very end gives the dish its flavor. My husband and I like our vegetables crisp-tender, but my kids like theirs cooked to death. So I take our portions out early and cook theirs longer. If you have a wok, please use it. Otherwise, a large, deep (at least 12-inch) nonstick skillet will do. You can even use an 8-quart pot.

## marinade

3 tablespoons tamari

3 tablespoons rice vinegar

2 tablespoons cornstarch

1 teaspoon sugar

1 teaspoon sesame oil

## stir-fry

2½ pounds boneless, skinless chicken thighs, trimmed of excess fat and sliced ¼ inch thick

2 tablespoons canola oil, plus more as needed

2 garlic cloves, minced

1 (12-ounce) bag broccoli florets (5 cups), cut into equal pieces

2 cups baby carrots, halved lengthwise

1 small onion, halved and sliced

2 cups chicken broth

1 tablespoon cornstarch

## seasoning sauce

2 tablespoons tamari

1 teaspoon sesame oil

1 teaspoon prepared pureed ginger

Cooked white or brown rice, for serving

**To make the marinade:** In a medium bowl, stir the 3 tablespoons of tamari, the rice vinegar, the 2 tablespoons of cornstarch, the sugar, and the 1 teaspoon sesame oil until smooth.

**To make the stir-fry:** Add the sliced chicken to the marinade and toss to coat well. Let rest for 10 minutes. Toss again just before frying. Heat the oil until very hot over medium-high heat in a wok, skillet, or very large pot. Add the marinated chicken in batches, stirring constantly. Cook until just cooked through and transfer to a large bowl.

When the chicken is cooked, add the garlic to the cooking pan, adding additional oil if needed, and cook, stirring, until translucent, but not browned, about 1 minute. Add the broccoli, carrots, and onion, and cook, stirring, for 2 minutes. Add 1 cup of the chicken broth, and cook, stirring, until the vegetables are crisp-tender, about 4 minutes.

In a small bowl, stir the 1 table-spoon of cornstarch into the remaining 1 cup of chicken broth. Add to the vegetables in the pan and cook, stirring, until the sauce thickens.

**Meanwhile, make the seasoning sauce:** Combine the 2 tablespoons tamari, the 1 teaspoon of sesame oil, and the pureed ginger and whisk well.

Return the chicken to the pan and add the seasoning sauce. Stir and cook until the chicken is heated through, 1 to 2 minutes. If you like your vegetables soft and tender, cook an additional 5 minutes. Serve over rice.

variations: Substitute sliced boneless beef sirloin or pork tenderloin for the chicken.

Substitute 2 pounds of peeled, deveined shrimp for the chicken.

# lemon chicken

## MAKES 8 SERVINGS

• • •

This is a kid-friendly riff on the Italian dish chicken piccata, which features garlic, olive oil, and fresh lemon. My family regards capers with suspicion, but yours may like them. If so, you can drain and add ¼ cup while cooking. Lemon chicken is easy to make and quick to cook, and the flavor is rich and fragrant, but the dish is not heavy.

**4 boneless, skinless chicken breasts (2 to 2½ pounds in all)**

**¼ cup extra virgin olive oil**

**1 teaspoon minced garlic**

**3 cups chicken broth**

**½ cup fresh lemon juice**

**Finely grated zest of 1 lemon**

**2 tablespoons cornstarch**

**Cooked white rice fettuccine or brown rice fettuccine, for serving**

**Chopped flat-leaf parsley, for garnish**

Starting at the thin end of one of the breasts, slice in half horizontally (as if butterflying the breast). You will now have two thin breast half slices. Cut each of those in half. Repeat with the remaining 3 chicken breasts. You will have 16 cutlets.

Flatten each cutlet between 2 pieces of plastic wrap to ¼ inch thick by pounding with a meat mallet or the back of a small frying pan. Uniform thickness is more important than uniform size and some tears are okay.

Pat the cutlets dry with paper towels. Heat 2 tablespoons of the oil in a 12-inch nonstick skillet over medium-high heat. Brown the cutlets, 4 at a time, first on one side, then on the other. Transfer the cutlets to an 8-quart pot with a lid. Add the remaining 2 tablespoons of olive oil halfway through the browning.

When all the cutlets are browned, remove the skillet from the heat and add the garlic, and stir. Return the skillet to the heat and deglaze with ¾ cup of the broth. Cook for 2 to 3 minutes, scraping the bottom of the skillet. Pour the deglazing liquid into the pot with the chicken cutlets, scraping with a silicone spatula.

Add 2 cups of the broth, and the lemon juice and zest to the pot; bring to a boil over medium-high heat. Decrease the heat, cover, and let simmer for 15 minutes.

In a small bowl, combine the cornstarch and the remaining ¼ cup of broth, stirring to a smooth paste. Add to the chicken and the broth in the pot, and cook, stirring gently, until the sauce thickens.

Serve over cooked white rice fettuccine or brown rice fettuccine. Garnish, if desired, with parsley.

# ten-minute barbecue sauce

## MAKES 3 CUPS

• • •

It doesn't get any easier than this: a 10-minute, no-cook barbecue sauce for Barbecue Baby Back Ribs (page 128) or Barbecue Pulled Pork or Chicken (page 126), or to use whenever you need a rich, tangy, Kansas City–style barbecue sauce. For a spicy sauce, add ⅛ to ¼ teaspoon of cayenne pepper. To store the sauce, transfer it to 1-cup containers with lids. Seal and refrigerate for up to 1 week. You can also freeze it. Whisk the defrosted sauce before using.

1 (6-ounce) can tomato paste

1 cup water

½ cup packed brown sugar

¼ cup cider vinegar

2 tablespoons gluten-free tamari

1 tablespoon molasses

1 tablespoon Dijon mustard

1 teaspoon garlic powder

1 teaspoon onion powder

1 teaspoon salt

¼ teaspoon liquid smoke

Place all the ingredients in the jar of a blender in the order listed. Cover and blend at low speed for 1 minute, scraping down the sides of the jar as necessary. Blend at high speed for 1 minute.

Alternatively, follow the recipe directions using a large bowl and a whisk. Whisk well to dissolve the brown sugar.

# barbecue pulled pork or chicken

## MAKES 5 PACKED CUPS, 10 TO 12 SANDWICHES

• • •

There are many 6- to 8-hour slow-cooker recipes for pulled pork, but this is a stovetop version that takes 2½ to 3 hours. The result is melt-in-your-mouth, fork-tender pork for barbecue sandwiches or to use in your favorite recipe for chili, tacos, quesadillas, and more. The recipe makes a lot, but it can be frozen in batches. You can substitute boneless, skinless chicken thighs for the Boston butt. The barbecue pulled chicken can be used in all the same ways as pork. To store the meat, transfer it to two 3-cup containers with lids. Drizzle enough of the reserved cooking liquid over the meat to moisten it well. Refrigerate for up to 4 days, or freeze.

**3 to 3½ pounds boneless Boston butt pork roast or 3 to 3½ pounds boneless, skinless chicken thighs**

**½ cup packed brown sugar**

**½ cup gluten-free tamari**

**¼ cup cider vinegar**

**1 cinnamon stick**

**1 tablespoon sweet Hungarian paprika**

**1 teaspoon garlic powder**

**½ teaspoon liquid smoke**

Trim the pork or chicken of large chunks of fat and discard the trimmings. (Kitchen scissors work well with chicken thighs.)

Place the pork or chicken in an 8-quart pot with a lid. Add all the ingredients in the order listed. Add water to cover. Pork usually takes about 3 quarts; chicken needs at least 2 quarts to balance the flavors.

Cover and bring to a boil over high heat. Decrease the heat to low and simmer, covered, until the meat is fork-tender: for pork, 2½ to 3 hours; for chicken 1½ to 2 hours.

Remove the pork or chicken to a large rimmed tray to catch the juices. Reserve 1½ cups of the cooking liquid. Using 2 forks, coarsely shred the pork or chicken. Transfer the meat to a serving dish and stir in the reserved cooking liquid.

**suggested uses:** For sandwiches, drain ⅓ to ½ cup of the pork or chicken using a slotted spoon. Serve on Hamburger Buns (page 49) drizzled with Ten-Minute Barbecue Sauce (page 125). You can also mix the drained meat with the sauce. Serve with Cole Slaw (page 137).

Add pulled pork or chicken to a Grilled Cheese Sandwich (page 104).

Substitute pulled pork or chicken for the ground meat in Chili con Carne (page 132).

Substitute pulled pork or chicken for the ground meat or sausage in Lasagna (page 116) or Spaghetti Pie (page 112).

Use pulled pork or chicken to top Pizza (page 113).

Add pulled pork or chicken to Basic Tomato Sauce (page 109) to top pasta.

Add pulled pork or chicken to tossed green salad or Pasta Salad (page 101).

Use pulled pork or chicken in your favorite taco recipe.

Add pulled pork or chicken to quesadillas (see page 82).

# barbecue baby back ribs

## MAKES 4 SERVINGS

● ● ●

Ribs became a top favorite gluten-free dinner at our house. When summer ended and the grill was retired for the season, I developed this recipe as a way to have ribs all year long. Now, when summer comes, I just finish the ribs on the grill. Each rack of ribs has 13 ribs. Any leftover ribs (not likely) can be reheated in the microwave on a microwave-safe plate for 2 minutes. These are great served with Cole Slaw (page 137).

**2 racks baby back ribs (4 to 4½ pounds total), cut into individual ribs**

**½ cup packed brown sugar**

**½ cup gluten-free tamari**

**¼ cup cider vinegar**

**1 cinnamon stick**

**1 tablespoon sweet Hungarian paprika**

**1 teaspoon garlic powder**

**1 teaspoon onion powder**

**1 cup Ten-Minute Barbecue Sauce (page 125) or barbecue sauce of choice, plus more for serving**

In an 8-quart pot, place the ribs, brown sugar, tamari, vinegar, cinnamon stick, paprika, garlic powder, and onion powder. Pour over enough water to cover (about 2 quarts). Place the lid on the pot and bring to a boil over high heat. Decrease the heat, and stir the ribs from the bottom to prevent sticking. Cover and simmer for 1½ hours, or until the ribs are fork-tender.

Remove the pot from the heat. Carefully remove the ribs and arrange on a rack that has been sprayed with nonstick cooking spray. Set the rack over a parchment paper–lined half sheet pan (18 by 13 inches). Let the ribs cool to room temperature. Brush the ribs with the barbecue sauce on all sides. The ribs can rest until ready to bake, or up to 1 hour.

Preheat the oven to 375°F. Bake the ribs for 15 to 20 minutes, until hot and bubbling and the barbecue sauce has browned, but not burned.

Serve with a dish of extra barbecue sauce.

variations: **TO DOUBLE THE RECIPE,** double the amount of ribs, but not the seasonings. Increase the pot size to 10 quarts, and add water to just cover. Prepare as directed.

To finish the ribs on the outdoor grill, cut each rack in half before cooking. Follow the recipe directions.

# meat-and-vegetable stew du jour

## MAKES 8 TO 10 SERVINGS

• • •

This is our family stew-of-the-day, which changes with whatever meat I have available. I don't recommend buying already cut-up "stew meat" from the market. Certain cuts, like the ones recommended here, do better with long, slow cooking, and the tender, juicy result is worth a little extra time and money. You can always ask the butcher to cut the meat up for you. Meat for stews is usually coated with wheat flour and browned, but gluten-free flour tends to stick, so browning it in a nonstick pan in batches works great.

**3 pounds boneless, skinless meat or poultry (Boston butt roast of pork, well-marbled chuck beef roast, chicken thighs, or turkey breast or thighs)**

**3 tablespoons canola oil**

**2 cups diced onions**

**2 garlic cloves, finely chopped**

**1 (6-ounce) can tomato paste**

**2 bay leaves**

**½ teaspoon salt**

**½ teaspoon freshly ground black pepper**

**4 cups beef broth (for beef) or chicken broth (for pork, chicken, or turkey)**

**1¼ cups water**

**2 cups red-skinned potatoes, peeled and cut into 1-inch cubes**

**2 cups baby carrots**

**1 (8-ounce) carton white mushrooms, stemmed and sliced**

**2 tablespoons cornstarch**

Cut the meat into 1½-inch pieces. Trim and discard large chunks of visible fat.

Heat the oil in a 12-inch nonstick skillet over medium-high heat. Cook the meat in batches until browned, turning with a spatula. Do not overcrowd the pan. Transfer the meat to an 8-quart Dutch oven (enameled iron works very well). Decrease the heat to medium.

When all the meat is browned, add the onions and garlic to the skillet. Cook over medium-high heat for 5 minutes, stirring occasionally. Transfer the onion mixture to the Dutch oven with the meat, stir in the tomato paste, bay leaves, salt, and pepper, and continue to cook for

5 minutes, stirring occasionally. Add the broth and 1 cup of the water, increase the heat to high, and bring to a boil, stirring to prevent sticking.

Decrease the heat to medium-low, cover, and simmer, stirring occasionally, until the meat is tender, about 1½ hours for beef or pork and 45 minutes for chicken or turkey. Add the potatoes, carrots, and mushrooms, and cook for another 30 minutes, or until tender. Remove the bay leaves and discard.

In a small bowl, combine the cornstarch and the remaining ¼ cup of water and stir until smooth. Add to the stew, stirring constantly, and cook until the stew thickens.

**note:** The stew may be made and refrigerated up to 4 days ahead, or frozen for up to 2 weeks. Reheat gently in a 350°F oven or on the stovetop in a hot water bath or with a heat diffuser. It may also be reheated in the microwave in small batches.

# taco pie

• • •

This is my version of traditional Mexican *chilaquiles*, a layered tortilla-chip concoction that I suspect developed as a way to use leftover chips, chicken, sauce, cheese, etc. I make this with leftover Barbecue Pulled Pork or Chicken (page 126) or plain cooked chicken (see page 91). There are endless variations. Be sure to use a traditional tomato-based salsa, not one with corn or beans or mango.

- **2 tablespoons canola oil**
- **½ cup finely chopped green onions, white parts only**
- **2 garlic cloves, minced**
- **1 (16-ounce) jar mild or spicy tomato-based salsa**
- **1 cup chicken broth**
- **8 ounces thick, restaurant-style yellow or white corn chips**
- **1½ cups shredded chicken (see page 91), or Barbecue Pulled Pork or Chicken (page 126)**
- **1 cup grated mozzarella or Monterey Jack cheese**
- **½ cup sour cream**
- **¼ cup finely chopped green onions, green parts only, for garnish**
- **¼ cup chopped fresh cilantro, for garnish**

Heat the oil in a 12-inch skillet over medium heat. Add the onions and garlic and cook, stirring, for 2 minutes, or until translucent, but not browned. Add the salsa and broth, and cook, stirring, until the sauce comes to a boil, 5 to 10 minutes. Add the corn chips and stir to soften.

When the chips are slightly softened, add the chicken or pork and the cheese and stir well. Cover and bring to a boil, shaking the pan occasionally.

Remove from the heat and let rest for 6 minutes. Uncover and dollop evenly with the sour cream. Sprinkle evenly with the green onions and cilantro, if desired. Serve with a large spoon.

**variations:** FOR A VEGETARIAN VERSION, substitute vegetable broth for the chicken broth, and 2 drained, rinsed (15-ounce) cans of black beans for the chicken or pork.

Substitute casein-free nondairy mozzarella cheese for the dairy cheese and nondairy sour cream for the dairy sour cream.

# chili con carne

## MAKES 4 QUARTS

• • •

*Chili con carne* literally means "chili peppers with meat." Beans were not originally a part of the dish, but red kidney beans have become a familiar component since the twentieth century. Beans, of course, give added protein. This chili is a main dish on its own, and the recipe makes enough for Nachos (page 81) and to freeze for another meal. Frozen in 1-quart covered containers, it will keep for up to 30 days. It is good made with ground beef, turkey, or chicken.

**2 tablespoons olive oil**

**3 pounds ground beef, turkey, or chicken**

**3 cups chopped onions**

**3 garlic cloves, minced**

**2 tablespoons chili powder**

**1 (6-ounce) can tomato paste**

**4 cups water**

**3 gluten-free bouillon cubes (beef for beef; chicken for turkey or chicken)**

**1 (28-ounce) can chopped tomatoes and their juice**

**3 (15½-ounce) cans red kidney beans, drained and rinsed**

**Chopped green onions, for garnish**

**Grated cheese or nondairy alternative, for garnish**

**Sour cream or nondairy alternative, for garnish**

**Sliced, canned, drained jalapeños, for garnish**

Heat the oil in an 8-quart pot over medium-high heat. Add the meat and cook, breaking up with a spatula, until browned. Add the onions and cook, stirring, until translucent, but not browned. Add the garlic and cook, stirring, for 2 minutes. Add the chili powder and stir to mix. Add the tomato paste and cook, stirring, for 2 minutes. Add the water, bouillon cubes, tomatoes, and beans. Bring to a boil. Decrease the heat, cover, and simmer, stirring occasionally, for 30 minutes.

Serve in bowls garnished with chopped green onions, grated cheese, a dollop of sour cream, and a few jalapeños, if desired.

# shrimp fried rice

## MAKES 6 TO 8 SERVINGS

• • •

Another restaurant favorite that I make at home, fried rice is a great way to use up leftover cooked rice. Good fried rice requires cold cooked rice, so I always cook more rice than I need for a meal. You don't need a wok to prepare this; I use a 12-inch round nonstick skillet. Leftovers can be refrigerated and heated in the microwave, so the dish travels well.

**2 tablespoons canola oil**

**½ cup finely chopped onion**

**2 teaspoons prepared pureed ginger (see Note)**

**2 teaspoons minced garlic**

**3 eggs, beaten**

**4 cups cold cooked long-grain white rice**

**3 tablespoons gluten-free tamari**

**1 teaspoon sesame oil**

**1 pound peeled, deveined, tail removed, frozen medium shrimp, defrosted**

**½ cup fresh orange juice**

**Chopped green onions, for garnish**

In a 12-inch nonstick skillet over medium heat, heat the oil. Add the onion and cook, stirring, until translucent, but not browned. Add the ginger and garlic and cook, stirring, for 1 minute. Add the eggs and scramble until cooked.

Add the rice, tamari, and sesame oil, and stir, breaking up the rice clumps with a potato masher.

Cook until the rice grains are separate and the rice is heated through. Add the shrimp and orange juice, and cook, stirring, just until the shrimp are opaque and cooked through.

Serve immediately garnished, if desired, with green onions. Refrigerate leftovers, covered, for up to 3 days.

note: Pureed ginger is available in Asian markets and most supermarkets in jars or tubes.

Chapter 5

# side dishes

Cole Slaw
Crispy Oven French Fries
Beef, Chicken, or Turkey Gravy
Applesauce
Baked Stuffing
Creamed Spinach
Mashed Potatoes or Sweet Potato Mash
Cheesy Scalloped Potatoes
Three-Bean and Corn Salad
Broccoli, Cauliflower, and Cheese

Side dishes may not be the star of a meal, but they still play an important role. What would turkey be without stuffing? Hamburgers without french fries? Mashed potatoes without gravy? Barbecue or fried chicken without Cole Slaw (page 137)?

Anyone can boil up a batch of frozen peas, corn, or green beans and have a perfectly respectable side dish. Believe me, I have many times, but my family never asks for encores. What they really like are side dishes they miss from restaurants, such as french fries. The recipe in this chapter for Crispy Oven French Fries (page 139) really produces crisp fries. They take a little work but almost no oil, and a $15 french fry cutter cuts the potatoes evenly and the work in half.

Gravy is one of the sides that my entire family missed when I could no longer thicken it with wheat flour. They were very happy with my solution, Beef, Chicken, or Turkey Gravy (page 140), and are even happier when I have a roasting pan to deglaze for the gravy. Stuffing is as much a part of Thanksgiving dinner as the turkey, and my gluten-free recipe is no more difficult to prepare than traditional stuffing.

There are special sides such as Creamed Spinach (page 144), a version of the famous Berghoff Restaurant spinach, Three-Bean and Corn Salad (page 147), and Applesauce (page 141). Of course, you can purchase applesauce in cans, jars, and plastic cups. But none of it tastes quite like homemade.

My kids will eat almost anything with cheese sauce, hence Broccoli, Cauliflower, and Cheese (page 148), and before we went gluten free, scalloped potatoes with cheese, milk, and flour were among their favorite sides. Gluten-free Cheesy Scalloped Potatoes (page 146) are an ideal stand-in.

# cole slaw

MAKES 6 TO 8 SERVINGS

● ● ●

Cole slaw from the deli counter at the grocery store is usually made with mayonnaise and other not always gluten-free ingredients. My kids love the mild, sweet-tangy flavor of this homemade vinegar-and-oil version, and it could not be simpler to prepare. If you like more dressing, prepare the larger quantity. If you like cole slaw lightly dressed, use the smaller measurements here to prepare a smaller amount of dressing.

¼ to ⅓ cup sugar

¼ to ⅓ cup rice vinegar

½ teaspoon salt

¼ to ⅓ cup canola oil

½ to 1 teaspoon celery seeds

1 (14-ounce) bag finely shredded cole slaw mix (cabbage and carrots)

In a small saucepan, combine the sugar, vinegar, and salt. Bring to a boil, decrease the heat, and cook, stirring, until the sugar is dissolved. Remove from the heat, add the oil and celery seeds, and stir.

Place the cole slaw mix in a 3-quart nonreactive bowl. Pour the dressing over the mix and toss well. Cover and refrigerate for at least 4 hours or overnight. Toss well before serving.

variation: Substitute 1 small head of very finely shredded green cabbage for the cole slaw mix. Prepare the larger amount of dressing.

# crispy oven french fries

• • •

Several chain restaurants offer gluten-free french fries, but the risk of cross-contamination is too big for us. So that leaves us with good but very expensive frozen french fries, or using a deep fryer and lots of oil (hard to store; unappetizing to reuse). This recipe produces crispy, downright cheap french fries, but you do need two things: a french fry cutter, to quickly cut the potatoes evenly, and an oven-safe metal rack. I use my cutter ($15 online) at least once a week, and the french fries cook more evenly. The dishwasher cleans up the rack, and I line the pan with foil. You can double the recipe.

**1½ pounds russet potatoes, peeled**

**2 tablespoons canola oil**

**½ teaspoon salt**

**Ketchup, for serving**

Preheat the oven to 450°F. Line a half sheet pan (18 by 13 inches) with foil. Place an oven-safe rack on the pan (or overlap 2 smaller racks to fit) and spray with non-stick cooking spray.

Square off the ends of the potatoes and cut them using a french fry potato cutter. Alternatively, use a knife to cut the potatoes into ⅜-inch batons as evenly as possible. Place the cut potatoes on a lint-free kitchen towel or paper towels and pat dry.

Transfer the potatoes to a large bowl. Add the oil and toss to coat well.

Place the potatoes evenly on the rack, not touching. Sprinkle evenly with a scant ½ teaspoon of salt. Bake until crisp and golden brown, 30 minutes.

Serve immediately, accompanied by a bowl of ketchup.

# beef, chicken, or turkey gravy

## MAKES 4 CUPS

• • •

What are mashed potatoes without gravy? Or turkey and stuffing without gravy? My kids like a lot of it, so here is a family-sized recipe. It freezes well, and you can easily halve the recipe. Increasingly, markets carry prepared turkey broth at Thanksgiving time. If you roast beef, chicken, or turkey, by all means, use the pan drippings and deglaze the pan with the broth (see Variation).

¼ cup (½ stick) butter or nondairy alternative

6 tablespoons Gluten-Free All-Purpose Flour (page 43) or flour of choice with xanthan gum in the mix

4 cups beef, chicken, or turkey broth

2 beef or chicken bouillon cubes

⅛ teaspoon liquid smoke (for beef gravy only)

In a 2-quart saucepan over medium-high heat, melt the butter. Add the flour and whisk to mix to a smooth paste. Cook, whisking, for 5 to 6 minutes, until the mixture is a definite light brown (not golden). Be careful not to burn.

Remove the pan from the heat. Add the broth and the bouillon cubes all at once. Whisk to mix. Return to medium-high heat and whisk constantly, being sure to reach the bottom and edges of the pan, until the mixture comes to a full boil and the bouillon cubes are dissolved.

Remove from the heat. If beef gravy, stir in the ⅛ teaspoon liquid smoke.

Serve immediately or cool in an ice water bath and refrigerate, covered, for up to 4 days. Freeze, in smaller containers, if desired, for up to 30 days.

variation: Substitute ¼ cup of pan drippings for the butter. Discard the excess fat in the roasting pan, then deglaze with broth before using the broth in the gravy.

# applesauce

• • •

Supermarket shelves are loaded with jars of applesauce, but I grew up eating my grandmother Carlyn's homemade applesauce—quite a cooking production involving a huge pot and a hand-cranked food mill. Now that I have my own family, I still make homemade applesauce—the easy way.

**3 pounds Granny Smith or Golden Delicious apples, cored, peeled, and cut into eighths**

**Juice of 1 lemon**

**1 cup water**

**⅓ cup packed brown sugar**

**¼ cup granulated sugar**

**½ teaspoon ground cinnamon**

**½ teaspoon salt**

Place all the ingredients in an 8-quart pot. Cover. Bring to a boil over high heat. Decrease the heat and simmer, covered, stirring occasionally from the bottom, until the apples are tender, about 30 minutes.

Remove the pot from the heat. Using a potato masher, mash the apples in the pot to your desired texture: chunky or smooth.

Serve warm, or transfer to a covered dish and refrigerate.

# baked stuffing

**MAKES 8 TO 10 SERVINGS**

• • •

Yes, you can make a great traditional stuffing for Thanksgiving and other turkey-time holidays using gluten-free White Sandwich Bread (page 45). It is best to add the bread cubes last and toss gently to mix, and to bake the stuffing separately rather than stuffing it into the bird. Feel free to vary the seasonings to suit your taste. Turkey broth is often available in supermarkets at Thanksgiving time. Leftover dressing can be refrigerated and reheated, covered, in the microwave or oven.

**8 cups 1-inch cubes White Sandwich Bread (page 45) or gluten-free bread of choice**

**4 celery ribs**

**4 medium onions, peeled**

**1 cup canola oil or butter**

**1 recipe breakfast sausage (see page 70) or 1 pound sausage of choice**

**2 cups turkey or chicken broth**

**1 tablespoon dried parsley**

**2 teaspoons rubbed sage**

**1 teaspoon poultry seasoning**

**1 teaspoon salt**

To toast the bread cubes, spread on a half sheet pan and bake in a 325°F oven until dry, about 30 minutes. Reserve and let cool.

Chop the celery and onions by hand, or else chop coarsely and place in the work bowl of a large-capacity food processor fitted with the steel blade and pulse in batches to chop.

Over medium heat in a 12-inch skillet, heat the canola oil or butter. Add the celery and onions and cook, stirring, until translucent and tender, but not browned. Remove the pan from the heat. Let the vegetables cool.

Meanwhile, spray a 10- to 12-inch skillet with nonstick cooking spray. Heat over high heat. Add the sausage and sauté, breaking up the clumps with a spatula,

until browned. Remove the pan from the heat. Let the sausage cool.

Preheat the oven to 350°F.

Place the vegetables and sausage in a 6-quart bowl. Stir to mix. Add the chicken broth and the dried parsley, sage, poultry seasoning, and salt. Add the toasted bread cubes and stir gently with a silicone spatula to mix.

Transfer the stuffing to a 9 by 13 by 2-inch baking dish lightly sprayed with nonstick cooking spray. Cover with foil sprayed on one side with nonstick cooking spray, sprayed side down. Bake until cooked through, 30 to 35 minutes. Remove the foil and bake for an additional 15 minutes to brown the top.

**variations:** Add 1 cup of chopped mushrooms to the vegetable mixture before sautéing.

Add 1 cup of chopped Granny Smith apples to the vegetable mixture before sautéing.

For a meatless stuffing, omit the sausage.

# creamed spinach

## MAKES 5 CUPS, 8 SERVINGS

● ● ●

Creamed spinach is a famous Berghoff Restaurant dish. The original recipe calls for half-and-half and flour. Here is a gluten-free version that is lower in fat, but not in flavor. Five cups is a lot, but it's hardly worth it to make less, because it disappears fast. You can also refrigerate the leftovers, covered, for up to 4 days and reheat them in the top of a double boiler.

**3 cups whole milk (regular or lactose free) or nondairy alternative (rice or soy)**

**1 chicken bouillon cube**

**½ teaspoon Tabasco sauce**

**½ teaspoon grated nutmeg**

**¼ teaspoon garlic powder**

**⅛ teaspoon celery salt**

**¼ cup (½ stick) unsalted butter or nondairy alternative**

**¼ cup All-Purpose Gluten-Free Flour (page 43) or flour of choice with xanthan gum in the mix**

**3 (10-ounce) packages frozen chopped spinach, thawed and squeezed dry (2½ cups)**

**½ cup crumbled crisp cooked bacon, for garnish**

In a 3-quart saucepan over medium heat, heat the milk, bouillon cube, Tabasco sauce, nutmeg, garlic powder, and celery salt to a simmer, stirring often. Remove from the heat and keep warm.

In another 3-quart saucepan, over low heat, melt the butter. Add the flour and whisk well to combine. Cook for 2 to 3 minutes, stirring often. Slowly whisk in the heated milk mixture, whisking constantly until smooth. Bring to a simmer and cook for 5 minutes, stirring constantly, until the mixture thickens. It will be very thick.

Stir in the spinach, stirring to mix well, and simmer for 5 minutes.

Serve hot. Garnish each serving with 1 tablespoon of the crumbled bacon, if desired.

# mashed potatoes or sweet potato mash

## MAKES 8 SERVINGS

• • •

Thank heavens for white and sweet potatoes, two satisfying, savory, and completely gluten-free foods. Here is a quick and easy way to cook and mash them in the same pot.

**3 pounds russet, Yukon gold, or sweet potatoes, peeled and cut into eighths**

**4 cups chicken broth**

**1 teaspoon salt**

**2 tablespoons butter or nondairy alternative**

**Pinch of ground cinnamon (for sweet potatoes only)**

**¼ cup packed brown sugar (for sweet potatoes only)**

Place the potatoes, broth, and salt in an 8-quart pot over medium heat and cover. Bring to a boil. Decrease the heat and simmer, covered, until the potatoes are very tender, 25 to 30 minutes.

Drain the potatoes, reserving all the liquid. Return the potatoes to the pot, and using a potato masher, mash well. Add 1 to 1½ cups of the reserved cooking liquid and whip with the potato masher until smooth. Add the butter and whip until melted. Serve warm, or keep warm in a hot water bath until ready to serve.

If using sweet potatoes, add the cinnamon and brown sugar and whip until the sugar melts.

variation: Whip ¼ cup of heavy cream or rice milk into the mashed cooked potatoes.

# cheesy scalloped potatoes

## MAKES 8 SERVINGS

• • •

Once baked, these layered potatoes cook unattended, stay warm for quite a while, and are just as good at room temperature—a great make-ahead side for a big dinner or buffet. Chicken broth provides all the salt needed and adds a rich flavor without extra calories. It is more important to cut the potatoes thinly and evenly than to cut whole slices. Use a mandoline, if you have one. Because potatoes vary in size, it is best to measure by weight for this dish.

**3 pounds russet potatoes, peeled and sliced ⅛ inch thick or thinner**

**1 medium onion, sliced paper-thin**

**1 cup (4 ounces) shredded aged Cheddar or Gruyère cheese**

**4 teaspoons potato starch (not flour)**

**2 cups chicken broth**

**½ cup (about 2 ounces) finely grated aged Parmesan cheese (see Notes)**

Preheat the oven to 375°F. Spray a 9 by 12 by 2½-inch pan with nonstick cooking spray.

Layer one-third of the potatoes in overlapping rows in the pan. Layer evenly with one-half of the onion. Sprinkle with one-half of the shredded cheese. Sprinkle evenly with 2 teaspoons of the potato starch. Repeat with a second layer of potatoes, onion, shredded cheese, and the remaining 2 teaspoons of potato starch. Top with a third layer of potatoes. Pour in the chicken broth, and sprinkle the top evenly with the grated Parmesan cheese.

Spray a 9 by 14-inch piece of foil with nonstick cooking spray. Place, sprayed side down, on the pan and crimp to seal the edges. Bake for 1 hour. Remove the foil and bake until the top is browned, 20 to 30 minutes.

Remove from the oven. Let cool for 15 minutes, or until cool enough to slice. Cut 2 by 4 for 8 servings. Serve warm or at room temperature.

**notes:** Grated Parmesan weighs differently depending on how finely it is grated.

Grate hard cheese in the food processor fitted with the steel blade; Cut the cheese into 1-inch chunks and pulse until finely crumbled.

# three-bean and corn salad

## MAKES 8 CUPS

• • •

My way to use leftover grilled corn and fresh-cooked green beans in summertime, when these vegetables are plentiful, was so popular with my family that I had to find a quick way to make it in wintertime. So I've included both canned and fresh vegetable options here. The one secret is to dry the canned or fresh vegetables of excess liquid that will dilute the salad dressing. This is best if you refrigerate it overnight before serving.

**1 (15-ounce) can green beans, drained and rinsed, or 1¾ cups cooked green beans cut into 1-inch lengths**

**1 (15-ounce) can corn kernels, drained and rinsed, or 1¾ cups kernels cut from fresh-cooked or grilled corn**

**1 (15-ounce) can cannellini or Great Northern beans, drained and rinsed**

**1 (15-ounce) can black beans, drained and rinsed**

**½ cup finely chopped onion**

**½ cup finely chopped celery**

**⅓ cup cider vinegar**

**⅓ cup sugar**

**⅓ cup canola or olive oil**

**1 teaspoon salt**

Line a half sheet pan (18 by 13 inches) with several thicknesses of paper towels and distribute the vegetables on the towels. Place two thicknesses of paper towels on top and pat dry. (If using leftover green beans and corn, add them to the beans and pat dry.)

In a small bowl, mix the vinegar and sugar and whisk to dissolve the sugar. Add the oil and salt and whisk to emulsify.

Place the vegetables in a large bowl, add the dressing, and toss well to mix. Transfer to a container with a tight-fitting lid and refrigerate overnight to meld the flavors. Toss before serving.

**variations:** Substitute 1 (15-ounce) can garbanzo beans, drained, for the green beans.

Substitute 1 additional (15-ounce) can cannellini or Great Northern beans, drained, for the green beans.

# broccoli, cauliflower, and cheese

**MAKES 8 SERVINGS**

• • •

My family will eat almost anything with Cheese Sauce (page 119) on it, including steamed broccoli and cauliflower. I buy already-cut florets in bags and steam them in the microwave. Then I either toss them in, or sauce them with, my cheese sauce. It is a quick, painless, appealing vegetable side dish. My kids like their vegetables so well done, I call them "dead." If your family will eat al dente vegetables (which I prefer), microwave only 3 to 4 minutes and voilà!

**1 (12-ounce) bag microwavable broccoli florets**

**1 (12-ounce) bag microwavable cauliflower florets**

**1½ to 2 cups Cheese Sauce (page 119), heated**

Place the bags of broccoli and cauliflower on a microwave-safe plate, and microwave according to the package directions to the desired degree of doneness.

Remove the vegetables from the bags and place in a large serving bowl. Add the cheese sauce and toss gently to cover. Alternatively, serve individual vegetable portions on plates and dollop with the hot cheese sauce.

Serve immediately.

# desserts

Easy-Mix Brownies
Chocolate Chip Cookies
Sugar Cookies
Oatmeal Cookies
Meringue Surprises
S'mores and More
Frosting and Filling for Cakes and Cupcakes
Yellow Cake and Cupcakes
Chocolate Cake and Cupcakes
Strawberry-Blueberry Shortcake with Chantilly Cream
First Try Apple Buckle Pie
Pat-in-the-Pan Pie Crust
Pumpkin Pie
Vanilla or Chocolate Pudding

There are three easy-schmeezy recipes in this chapter, and I suggest you prepare them first: Vanilla or Chocolate Pudding (page 171), S'mores and More (page 160), and First Try Apple Buckle Pie (page 166). The Frosting and Filling for Cakes and Cupcakes (page 161) is also a piece of cake. And if you begin with the recipe for Pat-in-the-Pan Pie Crust (page 168), a great Pumpkin Pie (page 167) is half done. If you like my Drop Biscuits (page 55) for breakfast, then you can jazz up the dough with lemon and sugar and create Strawberry-Blueberry Shortcake with Chantilly Cream (page 165) in the summer when berries are in season, or any other time of year using frozen berries.

Easy-Mix Brownies (page 153) do taste like chocolate and do not turn out gummy in the middle. The Chocolate Chip Cookies (page 154), Oatmeal Cookies (page 158), and Sugar Cookies (page 156) are all easy to mix and bake. These also all have a great shelf life (5 days if stored airtight), and they freeze and defrost well. Meringue Surprises (page 159) can be made with liquid egg whites, and they also have a long shelf life.

And now we come to the cakes and cupcakes. If you carefully follow the recipe methods and measure the ingredients exactly, you will be rewarded by a rich tender yellow cake or cupcakes (see page 163), and a moist chocolate cake or cupcakes (see page 164), all ready for frosting. And you will prove that you can bake your gluten-free cake and eat it, too!

Bolstered by success, you can ease into gluten-free dessert baking. Here are a few tips:

- Gluten-free doughs and batters are thick and sticky. When mixing in a stand mixer or in a bowl with a handheld mixer, if the batter becomes so thick it begins to crawl up the beaters, turn off the mixer, scrape down the beaters, and switch to mixing by hand with a silicone spatula.
- Gluten-free cakes sink and shrink. Do not be alarmed. The yellow or chocolate layer cake that puffed so high during baking will sink down and shrink from the sides of the pan as it cools. This happens with mixes as well as with homemade recipes. The cake will still taste good, be tender and moist, and look fabulous when frosted.
- Gluten-free doughs and batters do not automatically fill up baking pans side to side, nor do they level themselves. It is always necessary to spread the batter in the pan to the edges and then to level the top using a silicone spatula lightly oiled or sprayed with nonstick cooking spray.
- It is important to allow cake batter to rest for at least 5 minutes before baking. This is not to develop gluten; there is none. The purpose is to allow the dry ingredients to fully absorb the moisture in the liquid ingredients before baking.
- If a recipe flops the first time around, please go back and read the directions carefully and try again. I know a friend who failed at pancakes because she didn't let the batter rest for 5 minutes. And I myself have left out an ingredient (a fatal error) or omitted a step.

# easy-mix brownies

## MAKES 16 BROWNIES

• • •

Many gluten-free brownie recipes and mixes produce good chocolate flavor but a gummy texture—not these. Mix them directly in the pan after you melt the butter. Serve them plain, frosted (chocolate or vanilla frosting; see page 161), or dusted with confectioners' sugar, or add ½ cup mini chocolate chips or chopped walnuts or both. The recipe calls for my flour blend, which delivers a great result, but you can try other blends as long as there is xanthan gum in the mix.

½ cup (1 stick) butter or nondairy alternative (preferably Earth Balance)

½ cup confectioners' sugar

½ cup packed brown sugar

2 eggs

1 teaspoon vanilla extract

⅓ cup unsweetened cocoa powder (not Dutch process)

½ cup Gluten-Free All-Purpose Flour (page 43) or flour of choice with xanthan gum in the mix

2 teaspoons dried egg whites

¼ teaspoon baking powder

Pinch of salt

Preheat oven to 350°F.

In a 2-quart saucepan over medium heat, melt the butter. Remove the saucepan from the heat. Add the confectioners' sugar and brown sugar, and using a handheld beater, beat until smooth, scraping down the sides and the bottom of the pan as needed with a silicone spatula. Add the eggs and vanilla extract and beat until smooth. Scrape the sides and bottom of the saucepan.

Add the cocoa powder, flour, dried egg whites, baking powder, and salt. Beat on low until mixed, then beat on medium until the batter is smooth with no lumps. Scrape the sides and bottom of the saucepan as needed.

Spray an 8 by 8-inch baking pan with nonstick cooking spray. Line the bottom with parchment paper cut to fit. Spray the parchment. Using a sprayed or oiled silicone spatula, scrape the batter into the pan and level so the corners are filled and the top is even. Let the batter rest for 5 minutes before baking.

Bake until a wooden skewer inserted in the center comes up almost dry, 25 to 30 minutes. Remove from the oven and place on a rack to cool.

Remove from the pan and cut 4 by 4 into 16 squares.

# chocolate chip cookies

## MAKES 52 (2-INCH) COOKIES

• • •

A classic American cookie with hundreds of variations, chocolate chip cookies are one of the most missed cookies on the survey of teens for this book. This recipe has even been taste-tested on adults—who couldn't tell the difference from a cookie baked with wheat flour. I suggest refrigerating the dough for several hours or overnight to keep the cookies from spreading during baking. But thick or thin, the cookie is just as good. For this and all cookies, do not reload baking sheets hot from the oven with cookie dough. The dough will spread too quickly (see Note).

1 cup (2 sticks) butter or nondairy alternative, softened

1 cup packed brown sugar

½ cup granulated sugar

2 eggs

1 tablespoon molasses

2 teaspoons vanilla extract

2¼ cups All-Purpose Gluten-Free Flour (page 43) or flour of choice with xanthan gum in the mix

2 teaspoons dried egg whites

1 teaspoon baking powder

1 teaspoon baking soda

½ teaspoon salt

2 cups (12 ounces) chocolate chips or mini chocolate chips

1 cup chopped walnuts (optional)

Preheat the oven to 375°F. Line two 18 by 13-inch half sheet pans with parchment paper.

In a large bowl, beat the butter until light and fluffy. Add the brown and granulated sugars and beat until light and fluffy. One at a time, add the eggs, beating well after each addition. Add the molasses and vanilla extract and beat to mix.

Add the dry ingredients, except for the chips and walnuts, in the order listed and beat after each addition until the dough is smooth. Fold in the chips and walnuts, if using. Let the dough rest for 5 minutes.

Drop by rounded tablespoons, or with a leveled 1½-tablespoon cookie scoop, 2 inches apart on the prepared pans. Bake one pan at a time on the middle rack for 10 minutes, or until the cookies are golden brown and cooked through.

Remove the pan from the oven. Let the cookies rest on the pan for 5 minutes. Using a spatula, carefully transfer the cookies to a wire rack to cool completely.

Store in an airtight container with waxed paper or parchment between the layers for up to 5 days. Wrap individual cookies tightly in plastic wrap to freeze.

note: To cool hot baking sheets quickly, remove and reserve the parchment paper. Turn or angle each baking sheet, face down, in the sink and run cold tap water over the bottom for 30 seconds. Dry thoroughly, replace the parchment, and it's ready to bake again.

# sugar cookies

## MAKES 40 (2½-INCH) COOKIES

• • •

Sometimes you need a plain cookie like this to dunk in milk or tea, to eat with ice cream or pudding, to grab for a snack, or to pack for lunch. Don't use butter, or the cookies will spread too much while baking. The lemon juice acts as a leavening agent along with the baking soda, which also helps the cookies brown. A leveled 1½-tablespoon cookie scoop is the perfect size and makes for evenly baked, nicely shaped cookies. Stored in an airtight container, the cookies become soft and tender.

**1 cup nondairy solid shortening (preferably Earth Balance)**

**1 cup sugar, plus more for sprinkling**

**1 egg**

**Juice and finely grated zest of 1 medium or large lemon**

**2 tablespoons vanilla extract**

**2 cups Gluten-Free All-Purpose Flour (page 43) or flour of choice with xanthan gum in the mix**

**1 teaspoon baking powder**

**1 teaspoon baking soda**

**½ teaspoon salt**

Preheat the oven to 350°F. Line two 18 by 13-inch half sheet pans with parchment paper.

Place the shortening in the bowl of a stand mixer fitted with the whisk attachment and beat on medium speed until light and fluffy. Alternatively, use a medium bowl and a handheld mixer.

Add the sugar and beat on medium speed until the mixture is light and fluffy. Add the egg and beat until light and lemon colored. Add the lemon juice and the vanilla extract and beat to mix.

In a separate bowl, whisk together the flour, baking powder, baking soda, and salt. Add the flour mixture to the shortening mixture in 3 batches, beating after each addition until smooth. If using a handheld mixer, you may need to scrape down the beaters and use a large spoon for the last batch, as the dough will be thick. Add the lemon zest, and using a silicone spatula, stir to mix evenly. Let the dough rest for 5 minutes.

Drop by rounded tablespoons, or with a leveled 1½-tablespoon cookie scoop, 2 inches apart on the prepared pans. Sprinkle a pinch of sugar on the top of each cookie. The cookies will be mounded but will flatten slightly as they bake.

Bake one pan at a time for 16 minutes, or until the cookies are golden brown and cooked through. Remove the pan from the oven. Let the cookies rest on the pan for 2 minutes. Using a spatula, carefully transfer the cookies to a wire rack to cool completely.

Store the cooled cookies in an airtight container with waxed paper or parchment paper between the layers for up to 5 days, or freeze in small batches with waxed paper or parchment paper between the layers for up to 30 days.

variations: **FOR SNICKERDOODLE COOKIES,** sprinkle the cookies with Cinnamon Sugar (page 53) before baking.

**Omit the lemon zest and add 1 teaspoon of almond or coconut extract to the dough before baking.**

**Frost the baked, cooled cookies with Vanilla Glaze (page 58).**

# oatmeal cookies

• • •

The classic oatmeal cookie lends itself not only to raisins, but also to chocolate chips or chopped walnuts or pecans. There is no wrong choice. Just be sure the oatmeal comes from a dedicated gluten-free facility to avoid cross-contamination with wheat. A leveled 1½-tablespoon cookie scoop works best. No need to flatten the cookies; they spread during baking. You can mix the cookies, cover, and refrigerate the dough for up to 4 hours or overnight before baking.

1 cup (2 sticks) unsalted butter or nondairy alternative, at room temperature

1 cup packed brown sugar

2 eggs

2 teaspoons vanilla extract

1 teaspoon cider vinegar

1 cup Gluten-Free All-Purpose Flour (page 43) or flour of choice with xanthan gum in the mix

1 tablespoon dried egg whites

2 teaspoons ground cinnamon

½ teaspoon baking powder

½ teaspoon baking soda

¼ teaspoon ground allspice

½ teaspoon salt

1½ cups gluten-free old-fashioned rolled oats

½ cup dark or golden raisins, or mini chocolate chips, or chopped walnuts or pecans (optional)

Preheat the oven to 375°F. Line two 18 by 13-inch half sheet pans with parchment paper.

In a medium bowl, beat the butter and brown sugar together until light and creamy. Add the eggs and beat until light and fluffy. Add the vanilla extract and vinegar and beat to mix.

Add the flour, dried egg whites, cinnamon, baking powder and bakingsoda, allspice, and salt. Beat well. Beat in the oats and fold in the raisins, if using, or chips or nuts. Let the dough rest for 5 minutes.

Drop by rounded tablespoons, or with a leveled 1½ tablespoon cookie scoop, 2 inches apart on the prepared pans. Bake one pan at a time on the middle rack for 11 to 12 minutes, until the cookies are puffed and golden.

Remove the pan from the oven. Let the cookies rest on the pan for 3 minutes. Using a spatula, carefully transfer the cookies to a wire rack to cool completely.

Store in an airtight container with waxed paper or parchment paper between the layers for up to 5 days. Wrap individual cookies tightly in plastic wrap to freeze.

variations: Dust the cooled cookies with confectioners' sugar.

Frost the cooled cookies with Vanilla Glaze or Chocolate Glaze (page 58).

# meringue surprises

## MAKES 48 COOKIES

• • •

When I was a child, my favorite aunt, Vita, baked these cookies overnight using only the heat from the pilot in her old-fashioned gas oven. I still make them today for my kids, but rather than using whole eggs and wondering what to do with the yolks, I use prepared refrigerated egg whites. Be sure to let these egg whites warm slightly in the bowl at room temperature for about 20 minutes before beating. Make sure the bowl is clean, dry, and oil free.

**4 egg whites or equivalent prepared refrigerated egg whites**

**½ teaspoon cream of tartar**

**¼ teaspoon salt**

**¾ cup sugar**

**¾ teaspoon vanilla extract**

**1½ cups chocolate chips (preferably mini chips)**

**½ cup finely chopped pecans (optional)**

Preheat the oven to 200°F. Line two 18 by 13-inch half sheet pans with parchment paper.

Pour the egg whites into the bowl of a stand mixer fitted with the whisk attachment or use a large bowl and a handheld electric mixer. Beat the egg whites on low speed until they are foamy. Add the cream of tartar and salt. Beat on high speed until the egg whites form soft peaks. Add the sugar, 1 tablespoon at a time, mixing on high speed and scraping the sides of the bowl as necessary. Beat until stiff peaks form. Gently mix in the vanilla extract and chips, and the pecans, if desired.

Drop the batter by rounded tablespoons about 1 inch apart onto the prepared pans.

Bake for 1½ hours. Turn off the oven. Do not open the oven door. Let the meringues rest in the residual heat for 1 hour. Remove the baking sheets from the oven. Let the meringues cool completely on the pans to room temperature. Carefully lift them off with a thin spatula.

Store in large, covered, airtight containers between layers of waxed paper or parchment paper for up to 5 days. Do not freeze.

# s'mores and more

● ● ●

In the summer, I grill the s'mores I remember from my girls' and my Girl Scout days. The rest of the year, I make them in the oven. Today, there are several brands of gluten-free graham crackers on the market, some square and some round. Either will work.

**24 square or round gluten-free graham crackers**

**12 (2-inch) chocolate squares**

**12 large marshmallows**

**Grilled s'mores:** Preheat the grill. On a serving platter, assemble the s'mores: Top 12 of the graham crackers with 1 chocolate square each. Place a marshmallow on a long wooden skewer and toast over the grill until golden brown. Scrape the marshmallow on top of a chocolate square and top with a second graham cracker. Serve immediately. Repeat with the remaining ingredients.

**Oven-baked s'mores:** Preheat the oven to 400°F. Place 12 of the graham crackers on an 18 by 13-inch half sheet pan. Place 1 chocolate square on each. Top each with 1 marshmallow. Bake just until the chocolate and marshmallow melt, 5 to 6 minutes. Remove from the oven and top each with a second graham cracker. Serve immediately.

variations: Replace each chocolate square with 1 tablespoon of smooth or chunky peanut butter.

Place 1 banana slice between the chocolate and marshmallow.

# frosting and filling for cakes and cupcakes

## MAKES 3 CUPS

• • •

For cakes and cupcakes (and cookies), this basic frosting and filling can be flavored in several different ways and can be frozen for later use. Some confectioners' sugar contains casein, a milk protein, so read the ingredients if you need to avoid casein. This recipe makes enough to frost the tops and sides of two single-layer 8- or 9-inch round cakes, and also to fill the middle for a layer cake. It will frost the top of an 8- or 9-inch square or 9 by 13 by 2-inch cake with frosting to spare. When choosing flavoring extracts, always choose pure extracts, not imitation flavors, and check the labels to make sure they are gluten free.

**4 cups confectioners' sugar**

**⅛ teaspoon salt**

**¼ cup milk or nondairy alternative (almond, rice, or soy)**

**½ cup (1 stick) unsalted butter or nondairy alternative, softened**

**2 teaspoons vanilla extract**

**⅛ teaspoon almond extract**

Sift the sugar and salt into a 3-quart bowl. Add the milk, butter, and vanilla and almond extracts. Using a handheld mixer, beat on low to combine. Increase the speed and beat until the frosting is smooth. If needed, add more milk 1 tablespoon at a time to achieve the desired consistency. The frosting will thicken when refrigerated.

**variations:** TO MAKE CHOCOLATE FROSTING, add ½ cup of unsweetened cocoa powder to the confectioners' sugar before mixing.

Substitute the vanilla extract with a pure extract of almond, chocolate, lemon, orange, or peppermint.

Add 1 teaspoon of finely grated lemon or orange zest to the frosting.

# yellow cake and cupcakes

### MAKES 2 (9-INCH ROUND) LAYERS, OR 24 CUPCAKES

● ● ●

Yes, there can be fluffy, feather-light, tender yellow layer cake (the kind Sarah always calls "birthday cake") if you follow this simple recipe. The layers turn out level and firm enough for frosting, but light enough to yield to the touch of a fork. The secret? Heavy cream in place of fat in another form: butter, sour cream, or cream cheese.

**3 eggs**

**1½ cups sugar**

**1⅓ cups heavy cream**

**1 tablespoon vanilla extract**

**1 teaspoon cider vinegar**

**2 cups Gluten-Free All-Purpose Flour (page 43) or flour of choice with xanthan gum in the mix**

**2 teaspoons baking powder**

**1 teaspoon baking soda**

**½ teaspoon salt**

**1 recipe Frosting and Filling for Cakes and Cupcakes (page 161)**

Preheat the oven to 350°F. Spray two 9-inch round metal cake pans with nonstick cooking spray. Line the bottoms with parchment paper cut to fit. Spray the parchment lightly.

In a medium bowl, beat the eggs until light and lemon colored. Add the sugar and beat until light and fluffy. Add the heavy cream and beat until light and smooth. Add the vanilla extract and vinegar. Beat to mix.

In a separate medium bowl, combine the flour, baking powder, baking soda, and salt. Whisk to mix. Add the dry ingredients to the wet ingredients in 3 batches, beating well to form a smooth batter. If the batter becomes too thick for the mixer, scrape down

the blades and finish mixing with a large spoon or silicone spatula.

Divide the batter evenly, spoonful by spoonful, between the 2 cake pans. Smooth and level the top with a spatula that has been sprayed with nonstick cooking spray. Let rest for 5 minutes.

Bake for 25 to 30 minutes, until a cake tester inserted in the middle comes out clean.

Remove the pans from the oven and place on a wire rack to cool. When completely cool, run a spatula around the edges of each cake layer and invert onto a plate. Turn, right side up, onto a wire rack.

Frost the cake. Cut into wedges.

variation: **TO MAKE CUPCAKES:** Prepare the cake batter. Spray a 12-cup muffin pan with nonstick cooking spray. Insert paper cupcake liners and lightly spray the insides of the liners. Fill the cupcake liners two-thirds full with batter. Bake for 18 to 20 minutes, until cooked through and a cake tester inserted in the middle comes out clean. Let the cupcakes cool to room temperature. Remove the cupcakes from the pan and frost the tops. Repeat until all the batter is used. You should have about 24 cupcakes.

# chocolate cake and cupcakes

## MAKES 2 (8-INCH) ROUND LAYERS, OR 12 CUPCAKES

• • •

Rich but tender, chocolaty but not gummy, this cake is made for chocolate lovers. I like to frost only the middle and top with vanilla-flavored Frosting and Filling for Cakes and Cupcakes (page 161), but if you love chocolate, try the chocolate frosting as well.

**1 cup Gluten-Free All-Purpose Flour (page 43) or flour of choice with xanthan gum in the mix**

**½ to 1 cup unsweetened cocoa (not Dutch process)**

**4 teaspoons dried egg whites**

**½ teaspoon baking powder**

**½ teaspoon baking soda**

**¼ teaspoon salt**

**1 cup (2 sticks) butter or nondairy alternative, melted**

**2 teaspoons vanilla extract**

**4 eggs**

**1 cup confectioners' sugar**

**1 cup packed brown sugar**

**1 recipe Frosting and Filling for Cakes and Cupcakes (page 161)**

**Ice cream or whipped cream, for serving**

Preheat the oven to 350°F. Spray two 8-inch round metal cake pans with nonstick cooking spray. Line the bottoms with parchment paper cut to fit. Spray the parchment lightly.

Place the flour, cocoa, dried egg whites, baking powder, baking soda, and salt in a medium bowl and whisk to mix well.

Place the butter in a separate medium bowl. Add the vanilla extract and the eggs, one by one, beating well after each addition with a handheld mixer. Add the flour mixture and the confectioners' and brown sugars to the wet ingredients in batches, beating between each addition to mix. If the batter becomes too thick for the hand mixer, scrape

the beaters down, and mix well with a large spoon.

Divide the batter evenly, spoonful by spoonful, between the 2 cake pans. Smooth and level the top with a spatula that has been sprayed with nonstick cooking spray. Let rest for 5 minutes.

Bake for 30 to 35 minutes, until a cake tester inserted in the middle comes out clean. Remove the pans from the oven and place on a wire rack to cool. When completely cool, run a spatula around the edges of each cake layer and invert onto a plate. Turn, right side up, onto a wire rack.

Frost the cake. Cut into wedges and serve with a scoop of ice cream or a dollop of whipped cream, if desired.

**variation:** **TO MAKE CUPCAKES:** Prepare the cake batter. Spray a 12-cup muffin pan with nonstick cooking spray. Insert paper cupcake liners and lightly spray the insides of the liners. Fill the cupcake liners two-thirds full with the batter. Bake for 20 minutes, or until the cupcakes are cooked through and a cake tester inserted in the middle comes out clean. Let cool to room temperature. Remove the cupcakes from the pan and frost the tops.

# strawberry-blueberry shortcake with chantilly cream

## MAKES 9 SERVINGS

• • •

In the summer, I use fresh, lightly sweetened strawberries and blueberries; all other seasons, I prepare this family favorite with thawed frozen sweetened berries. The shortcakes are simply my morning Drop Biscuits (page 55) with grated lemon zest added to the batter and sugar sprinkled on top.

### shortcakes

Finely grated zest of 1 lemon

1 recipe drop biscuit dough (see page 55)

Sugar as needed for topping

### berry filling

2 pints fresh strawberries, hulled and halved, or 2 (16-ounce) bags frozen whole unsweetened strawberries, halved and defrosted

2 pints fresh blueberries, or 2 (16-ounce) bags frozen whole blueberries, defrosted

½ cup sugar

### chantilly cream

2 cups heavy cream

½ cup sugar

1 teaspoon vanilla extract

**To make the biscuits:** Stir the lemon zest into the biscuit dough, and sprinkle ½ teaspoon of sugar on top of each biscuit before baking according to the recipe directions.

**To make the berry filling:** In a large bowl, combine the berries and sugar. Stir gently to mix. Cover and refrigerate until ready to use. The longer the berries macerate, the sweeter and juicier they become.

**To make the Chantilly cream:** In a medium bowl, whip the cream, sugar, and vanilla extract together until firm. Cover and refrigerate for at least 1 hour.

**To assemble:** Slice each biscuit in half horizontally using a serrated knife. Place the bottom half of each biscuit in a serving bowl. Top with ½ cup of the berry filling. Spoon Chantilly cream generously over the berries. Cover with the top half of the biscuit. Divide any remaining berry filling equally among all the bowls and spoon it around the bottom of the shortcakes. Serve immediately.

variations: Substitute all strawberries for the blueberries.

Substitute raspberries for half the blueberries.

# first try apple buckle pie

## MAKES 1 (9- OR 10-INCH) PIE, 8 SERVINGS

● ● ●

Sarah had just been diagnosed with celiac disease and was dying for a piece of apple pie. I had no recipe then for pie crust, so I created this from scratch, and when Sarah ate it, she named it "First Try Pie." It is more like a buckle, a family of traditional American desserts made from seasonal fruit and consisting of a single cakelike fruit layer and a streusel top that "buckles" when baked. Thus, this apple buckle doubles for a pie, yet requires no crust, and can be served warm, room temperature, or cold. A scoop of ice cream or a dollop of whipped cream? Couldn't hurt.

### apples

- 2 to 2½ pounds Golden Delicious, Gala, or Jonathan apples, cored and peeled
- 3 teaspoons ground cinnamon
- 1 teaspoon ground allspice

### streusel

- ⅓ cup Gluten-Free All-Purpose Flour (page 43) or flour of choice with xanthan gum in the mix
- ¼ cup packed brown sugar
- ⅓ cup sliced almonds
- 3 tablespoons unsalted butter, melted, or nondairy alternative (preferably Earth Balance)

### batter

- ½ cup Gluten-Free All-Purpose Flour (page 43) or flour of choice with xanthan gum in the mix
- ½ cup sugar
- ½ teaspoon salt
- ½ cup milk (regular or lactose free) or nondairy alternative (almond, rice, or soy)
- 3 eggs
- 2 tablespoons melted butter or nondairy alternative
- 1 teaspoon almond extract
- 1 teaspoon vanilla extract

Lightly sweetened whipped cream or vanilla ice cream, for serving

Preheat the oven to 350°F. Spray a 9- or 10-inch glass pie plate with nonstick cooking spray.

**To make the apples:** Cut the cored apples in half lengthwise, then in quarters, then in eighths. You will need 4 cups of sliced apples. In a medium bowl, toss the apples with the cinnamon and allspice.

**To make the streusel:** Put the flour, brown sugar, sliced almonds, and butter in a small bowl and stir until well mixed and crumbly.

**To make the batter:** Put the flour, sugar, and salt in a medium bowl and whisk to mix. In a separate medium bowl, combine the milk, eggs, melted butter, and almond and vanilla extracts and beat with a handheld mixer until smooth. Gradually add the wet ingredients to the dry ingredients, beating with the mixer until the batter is smooth.

**To assemble:** Evenly distribute the apples in the prepared pie plate. Pour the batter evenly over the apples. Drop the streusel by the teaspoonful evenly over the batter.

Bake for 45 minutes, or until the buckle is puffed and golden and cooked through. Remove from the oven and let cool on a wire rack for 20 minutes. Slice into 8 wedges.

Serve warm or at room temperature, plain or garnished with a dollop of whipped cream or a scoop of ice cream.

# pat-in-the-pan pie crust

### MAKES 1 (9-INCH) PIE CRUST

● ● ●

Pie crusts are tricky to roll and transfer into a pan using a standard wheat flour recipe. Gluten-free pie crusts are even harder to handle. Here is my no-roll, pat-in-the-pan crust. For optimal crispness, pie crusts should be blind-baked, and this is no exception. Shape this dough as if you were working with clay, and if you make a hole, patch it. Fill the pie with your favorite sweet or savory filling and bake according to package or recipe directions.

**1½ cups Gluten-Free All-Purpose Flour (page 43) or flour of choice with xanthan gum in the mix**

**1 teaspoon salt**

**½ cup canola oil**

**1 large egg**

**1 teaspoon cider vinegar**

Preheat the oven to 425°F.

In the bowl of a food processor fitted with the steel blade, pulse the flour and salt to mix. In a cup with a spout, beat the oil, egg, and vinegar. With the processor running, pour the liquid through the feed tube and process just until a dough forms. It will be crumbly.

Turn a 9-inch pie pan face down and shape a 12-inch square piece of foil over the bottom. Remove the foil, preserving the shape, and set it aside.

Transfer the dough to the 9-inch pie pan, and using your fingers and the heel of your hand, press the dough evenly over the bottom and up the sides of the pie pan. Extend the dough slightly over the lip of the pie pan and shape it into a rim.

Fit the reserved foil shape into the pie pan over the crust and fill it with dried beans. Bake for 18 minutes, or until the crust is set and the rim is lightly golden. Remove from the oven and set on a rack to cool, leaving the foil and beans inside. After 15 minutes, carefully remove the foil and beans and let the pie crust cool to room temperature.

tips: Setting the pie pan on a half sheet pan to bake makes it easy to put it in and get it out of the oven.

Setting the pie pan on top of a silicone heatproof pad or pot holder keeps the pie from slipping.

# pumpkin pie

• • •

At our house, pumpkin pie is not just for Thanksgiving. We start baking it whenever summer changes to fall. Individual wedges freeze well in airtight plastic containers. A 9-inch pie shell, which is based on one 15-ounce can of pumpkin, doesn't hold all the pumpkin filling, so I spray two 8-ounce ramekins with nonstick cooking spray and divide the extra filling between them. My kids call these "pumpkin puddings." Both are great served with whipped cream or vanilla ice cream.

**1 Pat-in-the-Pan Pie Crust (page 168), prebaked**

**1 (15-ounce) can pumpkin (not pumpkin pie filling)**

**1 (12-ounce) can evaporated milk**

**⅔ cup packed brown sugar**

**2 eggs**

**1½ teaspoons pumpkin pie spice**

**¼ teaspoon salt**

Preheat the oven to 375°F. Place the pan with the prebaked pie crust on an 18 by 13-inch half sheet pan. Spray two 8-ounce ovenproof ramekins with nonstick cooking spray.

In a medium bowl, beat the canned pumpkin, evaporated milk, brown sugar, eggs, pumpkin pie spice, and salt until very smooth and well mixed. Fill the pie crust to the rim. Divide the excess filling between the ramekins. Place the ramekins on a sheet pan beside the pie.

Bake for 40 to 50 minutes, until the pie is puffed and cooked through in the center. Remove from the oven and let cool on a wire rack.

Cut into wedges and serve.

**variations:** FOR A NONDAIRY PIE, substitute almond, rice, or soy milk for the evaporated milk.

FOR A CREAMIER PIE, substitute 1½ cups heavy cream or half-and-half for the evaporated milk.

# vanilla or chocolate pudding

## MAKES 4 SERVINGS

• • •

Pudding is simple, easy, quick, and naturally gluten free, and I have always made my own. This pudding calls for 1 egg and a little unflavored gelatin to help the texture, is foolproof, and can be made lactose- or dairy-free. Be sure to whisk the refrigerated pudding until smooth before serving, because all cornstarch puddings tend to separate over time.

½ cup sugar

3 tablespoons cornstarch

½ teaspoon unflavored gelatin

¼ teaspoon salt

1 egg

2 cups whole milk (regular or lactose free) or nondairy alternative (almond, rice, or soy)

2 tablespoons butter or nondairy alternative

1 tablespoon vanilla extract

Fresh berries and whipped cream or Marshmallow Fluff, or chocolate or caramel syrup, for serving

In a 2-quart saucepan, combine the sugar, cornstarch, gelatin, and salt and whisk well.

In a medium bowl, beat the egg well with a whisk, then add the milk, whisking to mix.

Add ½ cup of the milk mixture to the dry mixture and whisk until the mixture forms a smooth paste with no lumps. Add the remaining milk mixture and whisk well. Cook over medium heat, whisking the bottom and edges of the pan constantly, until the pudding just begins to boil and becomes thick and glossy, about 8 minutes.

Remove from the heat and whisk in the butter and vanilla extract until well mixed. Cool the pudding in an ice-water bath, stirring to speed the cooling.

Place plastic wrap on the surface of the pudding to prevent a skin from forming. Refrigerate until cold. Spoon into individual dessert dishes. Garnish with berries and whipped cream or Marshmallow Fluff, or drizzle with chocolate or caramel syrup.

The pudding will keep for up to 4 days in the refrigerator. Whisk smooth before serving.

**variations:** **TO MAKE BANANA PUDDING,** layer sliced bananas and the pudding in a parfait dish. Top with whipped cream or Marshmallow Fluff.

**FOR CHOCOLATE PUDDING,** increase the sugar to ⅔ cup and whisk ¼ cup of unsweetened cocoa into the dry ingredients. Proceed with the recipe instructions.

# acknowledgments

To Sarah: Through your health challenge, we have created an opportunity for your voice to be heard around the world to calm, educate, and give hope to the newly diagnosed. How proud I am of how you have grown beyond your illness. I love you.

To my husband, Jim McClure, and my children Lindsey and Todd for tasting, retasting, and living supportively in a gluten-free household.

To Dr. Suzanne Nelson for taking such good care of Sarah—then and now. You're the best!

To Betsy Hjelmgren, MS, RD, LD, CSP, for guiding Sarah through her new diet and making sure the recipes in the cookbook were gluten free.

To Wednesdays with Nancy Ryan: What a blessing it has been to play in your kitchen, listen to your wisdom, laugh about the failures, and celebrate the successes, especially nailing recipes on our first try. Thank you for your patience, knowledge, and get-it-done force.

To John Ryan, the master of gluten-free grocery shopping for recipe testing!

To Ashley Malmquist, who tested the recipes and was only stumped by rolling spring rolls.

To the University of Chicago Celiac Disease Center, my gratitude for their support and my admiration for their ongoing research and dedication.

To my agent, Lisa Ekus, for our third time around: You roll with the punches and see me through thick and thin.

To my publisher, Andrews McMeel, and Kirsty Melville, for our third time around, and our talented editor there, Lane Butler, who took the manuscript and made it a book—a thousand thanks!

# metric conversions and equivalents

## metric conversion formulas

| to convert | multiply |
|---|---|
| Ounces to grams | Ounces by 28.35 |
| Pounds to kilograms | Pounds by .454 |
| Teaspoons to milliliters | Teaspoons by 4.93 |
| Tablespoons to milliliters | Tablespoons by 14.79 |
| Fluid ounces to milliliters | Fluid ounces by 29.57 |
| Cups to milliliters | Cups by 236.59 |
| Cups to liters | Cups by .236 |
| Pints to liters | Pints by .473 |
| Quarts to liters | Quarts by .946 |
| Gallons to liters | Gallons by 3.785 |
| Inches to centimeters | Inches by 2.54 |

## common ingredients and their approximate equivalents

1 cup uncooked white rice = 185 grams
1 cup all-purpose flour = 140 grams
1 stick butter
    (4 ounces • ½ cup • 8 tablespoons) = 110 grams
1 cup butter
    (8 ounces • 2 sticks • 16 tablespoons) = 220 grams
1 cup brown sugar, firmly packed = 225 grams
1 cup granulated sugar = 200 grams

## oven temperatures

To convert Fahrenheit to Celsius, subtract 32 from Fahrenheit, multiply the result by 5, then divide by 9.

| description | fahrenheit | celsius | british gas mark |
|---|---|---|---|
| Very cool | 200° | 95° | 0 |
| Very cool | 225° | 110° | ¼ |
| Very cool | 250° | 120° | ½ |
| Cool | 275° | 135° | 1 |
| Cool | 300° | 150° | 2 |
| Warm | 325° | 165° | 3 |
| Moderate | 350° | 175° | 4 |
| Moderately hot | 375° | 190° | 5 |
| Fairly hot | 400° | 200° | 6 |
| Hot | 425° | 220° | 7 |
| Very hot | 450° | 230° | 8 |
| Very hot | 475° | 245° | 9 |

Information compiled from a variety of sources, including *Recipes into Type* by Joan Whitman and Dolores Simon (Newton, MA: Biscuit Books, 2000); *The New Food Lover's Companion* by Sharon Tyler Herbst (Hauppauge, NY: Barron's, 1995); and *Rosemary Brown's Big Kitchen Instruction Book* (Kansas City, MO: Andrews McMeel, 1998).

## approximate metric equivalents

### volume

| | |
|---|---|
| ¼ teaspoon | 1 milliliter |
| ½ teaspoon | 2.5 milliliters |
| ¾ teaspoon | 4 milliliters |
| 1 teaspoon | 5 milliliters |
| 1¼ teaspoons | 6 milliliters |
| 1½ teaspoons | 7.5 milliliters |
| 1¾ teaspoons | 8.5 milliliters |
| 2 teaspoons | 10 milliliters |
| 1 tablespoon (½ fluid ounce) | 15 milliliters |
| 2 tablespoons (1 fluid ounce) | 30 milliliters |
| ¼ cup | 60 milliliters |
| ⅓ cup | 80 milliliters |
| ½ cup (4 fluid ounces) | 120 milliliters |
| ⅔ cup | 160 milliliters |
| ¾ cup | 180 milliliters |
| 1 cup (8 fluid ounces) | 240 milliliters |
| 1¼ cups | 300 milliliters |
| 1½ cups (12 fluid ounces) | 360 milliliters |
| 1⅔ cups | 400 milliliters |
| 2 cups (1 pint) | 460 milliliters |
| 3 cups | 700 milliliters |
| 4 cups (1 quart) | 0.95 liter |
| 1 quart plus ¼ cup | 1 liter |
| 4 quarts (1 gallon) | 3.8 liters |

### weight

| | |
|---|---|
| ¼ ounce | 7 grams |
| ½ ounce | 14 grams |
| ¾ ounce | 21 grams |
| 1 ounce | 28 grams |
| 1¼ ounces | 35 grams |
| 1½ ounces | 42.5 grams |
| 1⅔ ounces | 45 grams |
| 2 ounces | 57 grams |
| 3 ounces | 85 grams |
| 4 ounces (¼ pound) | 113 grams |
| 5 ounces | 142 grams |
| 6 ounces | 170 grams |
| 7 ounces | 198 grams |
| 8 ounces (½ pound) | 227 grams |
| 16 ounces (1 pound) | 454 grams |
| 35.25 ounces (2.2 pounds) | 1 kilogram |

### length

| | |
|---|---|
| ⅛ inch | 3 millimeters |
| ¼ inch | 6 millimeters |
| ½ inch | 1¼ centimeters |
| 1 inch | 2½ centimeters |
| 2 inches | 5 centimeters |
| 2½ inches | 6 centimeters |
| 4 inches | 10 centimeters |
| 5 inches | 13 centimeters |
| 6 inches | 15¼ centimeters |
| 12 inches (1 foot) | 30 centimeters |

# index

### • • • a • • •

additives, 27
All-Day Breakfast Sandwich, 71
allergic reactions, 16
   dairy products, 38
   lactose intolerance vs., 38
almond milk
   Chocolate Glaze, 58
   Cinnamon, Blueberry, or Chocolate
     Chip Muffins, 66
   Drop Biscuits, 55
   First Try Apple Buckle Pie, 166–67
   Fluffy Pancakes or Waffles, 52
   French Toast and French Toast
     Sticks, 54
   Frosting and Filling for Cakes and
     Cupcakes, 161
   nondairy Pumpkin Pie, 169
   nondairy Quiche, 68
   Vanilla Glaze, 58
   Vanilla or Chocolate Pudding, 171
almonds
   Almond–Sour Cream Coffee Cake,
     60–61
   First Try Apple Buckle Pie, 166–67
appetizers. See starters
apples
   Applesauce, 141
   Baked Stuffing, 142, 143
   First Try Apple Buckle Pie, 166–67
   Grilled Cheese Sandwich variation,
     104, 105
Asian
   Pork, Broccoli, and Carrot Stir-Fry,
     122–23
   Sarah's Spring Rolls, 84, 85–87
   Shrimp Fried Rice, 133
autoimmune conditions, 15

### • • • b • • •

bacon
   All-Day Breakfast Sandwich, 71
   Corn and Bacon Chowder, 93
   as garnish, 94, 104, 144
   Quesadillas and Beyond, 82
   Quiche, 68, 69

Baked Stuffing, 142, 143
bananas
   Banana Bread Squares, 67
   Banana Pancakes, 53
barbecue
   Barbecue Baby Back Ribs, 128
   Barbecue Pulled Pork or Chicken,
     126–27
   Taco Pie variation, 130, 131
   Ten-Minute Barbecue Sauce, 125
barley, 27
Basic Burgers or Meatballs, 102, 103
Basic Tomato Sauce, 109
beans, 26
   Chili Con Carne, 132
   Nachos, 80, 81
   Pasta Salad, 101
   Quesadillas and Beyond, 82
   Taco Pie variation, 131
   Three-Bean and Corn Salad, 147
   White Bean Dip, 78
beef
   Basic Burgers or Meatballs, 102, 103
   Beef, Broccoli, and Carrot Stir-Fry,
     122–23
   Beef, Chicken, or Turkey Gravy, 140
   Chili Con Carne, 132
   Lasagna, 116–17
   Meat-and-Vegetable Stew
     du Jour, 129
   Quesadillas and Beyond, 82
Berghoff Tastes-Like-Rye Bread, 50–51
berries
   Cinnamon, Blueberry, or Chocolate
     Chip Muffins, 66
   Strawberry Pancakes, 53
   Strawberry-Blueberry Shortcake
     with Chantilly Cream, 165
biopsy, 17–18
birthdays, 11–12. See also parties
biscuits, 55
bread machine, 24
   how to use, 44
breads
   Banana Bread Squares, 67
   Berghoff Tastes-Like-Rye Bread,
     50–51

Cinnamon-Raisin Bread and
   Cinnamon Buns, 64–65
Corn Bread, 59
Drop Biscuits, 55
Gluten-Free All-Purpose Flour, 43
Hamburger Buns, 49
Hot Dog Buns, 48
Pumpkin Bread Bars, 62
White Sandwich Bread, 45–47
breakfast
   All-Day Breakfast Sandwich, 71
   Almond–Sour Cream Coffee Cake,
     60–61
   Banana Bread Squares, 67
   Banana Pancakes, 53
   Breakfast Sausage Patties, 70
   Cheddar-Ham Quiche, 68
   Chocolate Chip Pancakes, 53
   Chocolate Glaze, 58
   Cinnamon, Blueberry, or Chocolate
     Chip Muffins, 66
   Cinnamon Sugar, 53
   Drop Biscuits, 55
   Fluffy Pancakes or Waffles, 52–53
   French Toast and French Toast
     Sticks, 54
   Glazed Baked Doughnuts, 56, 57
   gluten-free, 10, 13
   Pumpkin Bread Bars, 62
   Quesadillas and Beyond, 82
   Quiche, 68, 69
   Spinach Quiche, 68
   Strawberry Pancakes, 53
   Streusel Topping, 60–61
   Vanilla Glaze, 58
   Vanilla Sugar, 63
   Vegetable Quiche, 68
Broccoli, Cauliflower, and Cheese, 148
broth, chicken, 91
brown rice flour, 43
brown rice pasta, 101, 110, 111,
   116, 118
brownies, Easy-Mix Brownies, 153
burgers
   Basic Burgers or Meatballs, 102, 103
   hamburger bun pan, 24
   Hamburger Buns, 49

### c

cakes
  Almond–Sour Cream Coffee Cake,
    60–61
  Cakes and Cupcakes Frosting and
    Filling, 161, 162
  Chocolate Cake and Cupcakes, 164
  Frosting and Filling for Cakes and
    Cupcakes, 161, 162
  Strawberry-Blueberry Shortcake
    with Chantilly Cream, 165
  Yellow Cake and Cupcakes, 163
cancer, 7, 15
celiac disease
  allergy vs., 16
  diagnosis, 7, 8, 17–18
  gold standard test for, 7
  newly diagnosed, 8
  symptoms, 7, 16–17
  treatment, 18
  in U.S. population, 3, 15
  what it is, 15–16
Celiac Disease Foundation, 9
cereals, 27
Cheddar-Ham Quiche, 68
cheese, 27. See also cream cheese
  All-Day Breakfast Sandwich, 71
  Broccoli, Cauliflower, and
    Cheese, 148
  Cheddar-Ham Quiche, 68
  Cheese Sauce, 119
  Cheesy Scalloped Potatoes, 146
  as garnish, 132
  Grilled Cheese Sandwich, 104
  Ham and Cheese Roll-Ups, 83
  Lasagna, 116–17
  Linguine Alfredo-Style, 111
  Macaroni and Cheese, 118
  Nachos, 80, 81
  nondairy, 22, 38, 118
  Pizza, 113–15
  Quesadillas and Beyond, 82
  Quiche, 68, 69
  Spaghetti Pie, 112
  Spinach Quiche, 68
  Taco Pie, 130, 131
  Tuna Salad or Tuna Melt, 100
  Vegetarian Pasta Salad, 101
  White Bean Dip, 78
chicken
  Barbecue Pulled Pork or Chicken,
    126–27

Basic Burgers or Meatballs, 102, 103
Beef, Chicken, or Turkey Gravy, 140
Chicken, Broccoli, and Carrot
  Stir-Fry, 122–23
Chicken Broth and Chicken Meat, 91
Chicken Noodle Soup, 92
Chili Con Carne, 132
Crispy Fish or Chicken, 120, 121
Ham and Cheese Roll-Ups, 83
Lasagna, 116–17
Lemon Chicken, 124
Meat-and-Vegetable Stew
  du Jour, 129
Pasta Salad, 101
Quesadillas and Beyond, 82
Taco Pie, 130, 131
Chili Con Carne, 132
chocolate, 27
  Chocolate Cake and Cupcakes, 164
  Chocolate Chip Cookies, 154, 155
  Chocolate Chip Pancakes, 53
  Chocolate Glaze, 58
  Chocolate Pudding, 170, 171
  Cinnamon, Blueberry, or Chocolate
    Chip Muffins, 66
  Easy-Mix Brownies, 153
  Vanilla or Chocolate Pudding,
    170, 171
chowder, 93
cinnamon
  Cinnamon, Blueberry, or Chocolate
    Chip Muffins, 66
  Cinnamon Sugar, 53
  Cinnamon-Raisin Bread and
    Cinnamon Buns, 64–65
Cole Slaw, 137
convenience foods, 9, 10, 22
cookies
  Banana Bread Squares, 67
  Chocolate Chip Cookies, 154, 155
  Easy-Mix Brownies, 153
  Oatmeal Cookies, 158
  Pumpkin Bread Bars, 62
  Sugar Cookies, 156–57
cooking, gluten free
  breakfast, 10, 13
  dinner, 10, 13
  lunch, 10, 13
  normal eating and, 9–10
  snacks, 13
corn
  Corn and Bacon Chowder, 93
  Corn Bread, 59

cornstarch, 43
  Three-Bean and Corn Salad, 147
cosmetics, as source of gluten, 27
cream cheese
  Almond–Sour Cream Coffee
    Cake, 60
  Green Onion Dip, 77
  Ham and Cheese Roll-Ups, 83
  Linguine Alfredo-Style, 111
Creamed Spinach, 144
Creamy Tomato Soup, 96
Crispy Fish or Chicken, 120, 121
Crispy Oven French Fries, 138, 139
Crohn's disease, 7

### d

dairy alternatives. See also almond
  milk; rice milk; soy milk
  nondairy cheese, 22, 38, 118
dessert
  Chocolate Cake and Cupcakes, 164
  Chocolate Chip Cookies, 154, 155
  Chocolate Pudding, 170, 171
  Easy-Mix Brownies, 153
  First Try Apple Buckle Pie, 166–67
  Frosting and Filling for Cakes and
    Cupcakes, 161, 162
  Meringue Surprises, 159
  Oatmeal Cookies, 158
  Pat-in-the-Pan Pie Crust, 168
  Pumpkin Pie, 169
  quesadillas for, 82
  S'mores and More, 160
  Strawberry-Blueberry Shortcake
    with Chantilly Cream, 165
  Sugar Cookies, 156–57
  Vanilla Pudding, 170, 171
  Yellow Cake and Cupcakes, 163
Deviled Eggs, 99
diabetes, 15
diagnosis, 7, 8, 17–18
dinner
  Baked Stuffing, 142
  Barbecue Baby Back Ribs, 128
  Barbecue Pulled Pork or Chicken,
    126–27
  Basic Burgers or Meatballs, 102, 103
  Basic Tomato Sauce, 109
  Beef, Chicken, or Turkey Gravy, 140
  Cheddar-Ham Quiche, 68
  Cheese Sauce, 119

Chicken, Broccoli, and Carrot
    Stir-Fry, 122–23
Chili Con Carne, 132
Corn Bread, 59
Crispy Fish or Chicken, 120, 121
Drop Biscuits, 55
eating away from home, 29–30, 31
gluten-free, 10, 13
Ham and Cheese Roll-Ups, 83
Italian Tomato Sauce, 109
Lasagna, 116–17
Lemon Chicken, 124
Linguine Alfredo-Style, 111
Macaroni and Cheese, 118
Meat-and-Vegetable Stew
    du Jour, 129
Pizza, 113–15
Quesadillas and Beyond, 82
Shrimp Fried Rice, 133
Spaghetti and Meatballs, 110
Spaghetti Pie, 112
Taco Pie, 130, 131
Ten-Minute Barbecue Sauce, 125
dips
    Green Onion Dip, 77
    Spinach Dip, 76
    Sweet Potato Fingers with
        Marshmallow Dip, 79
    White Bean Dip, 78
doughnuts
    doughnut pan, 24
    Glazed Baked Doughnuts, 56, 57
Drop Biscuits, 55

• • • **e** • • •

Easy-Mix Brownies, 153
environmental cross-contamination, 27

• • • **f** • • •

First Try Apple Buckle Pie, 166–67
fish
    Crispy Fish or Chicken, 120, 121
    Quesadillas and Beyond, 82
    Tuna Salad or Tuna Melt, 100
flour, 26–27
    brown rice flour, 43
    Gluten-Free All-Purpose Flour, 43
    potato starch flour, 43
    quinoa flour, 43
    sorghum flour, 43
    tapioca flour, 43

teff flour, 26, 50
    white rice flour, 43
Fluffy Pancakes or Waffles, 52–53
french fries
    Crispy Oven French Fries, 138, 139
    cross-contamination in, 27
    french fry cutter, 24
French Toast and French Toast
    Sticks, 54
Frosting and Filling for Cakes and
    Cupcakes, 161, 162
fruit, fresh, 6, 26
    Applesauce, 141
    Baked Stuffing, 142, 143
    Banana Bread Squares, 67
    Banana Pancakes, 53
    Cinnamon, Blueberry, or Chocolate
        Chip Muffins, 66
    First Try Apple Buckle Pie, 166–67
    Lemon Chicken, 124
    Strawberry Pancakes, 53
    Strawberry-Blueberry Shortcake
        with Chantilly Cream, 165

• • • **g** • • •

genetic susceptibility, 15
Glazed Baked Doughnuts, 56, 57
gluten
    by association, 27
    hidden sources of, 27
    what it is, 16
gluten-free diet
    100 percent, 19–20
    for all family members, 8–9, 18–19
    foods, 26
    for lactose intolerance, 38
    mainstream recognition of, 5
    mixes, 22
    recipe guidelines, 37
    top 30 foods most missed, 21
gluten-free kitchen
    equipment/food preparation
        surfaces, 24
    refrigerator/freezer, 22–23
    revolution toward, 9
    storage/pantry, 22
    suggestions for gluten-free zone,
        25–26
gluten full foods, 26–27
gluten sensitivity, 18
Gluten-Free All-Purpose Flour, 43
gluten-free prepared mixes, 22

grains, whole, 6
    brown rice pasta, 101, 110, 111,
        116, 118
    Chicken Noodle Soup variation, 92
    rice, 43, 85, 133
    rye, 27, 50–51
    Shrimp Fried Rice, 133
    teff, 26, 50
    wheat, 27
gravy, beef, chicken, or turkey, 140
green beans
    Three-Bean and Corn Salad, 147
    Vegetable Quiche, 68, 69
Green Onion Dip, 77
Green Tomatillo Quesadilla, 82
Grilled Cheese Sandwich, 104, 105
grocery shopping, 26
    hidden sources of gluten, 27
    Internet resources, 39
    Unsafe Foods List, 27

• • • **h** • • •

Ham and Cheese Roll-Ups, 83
hamburgers
    Basic Burgers or Meatballs, 102, 103
    hamburger bun pan, 24
    Hamburger Buns, 49
holidays
    Halloween, 6
    Thanksgiving stuffing, 142
    top 30 foods kids miss most, 21
Honey-Mustard Vinaigrette, 98
Hot Dog Buns, 24, 48
Hummus, 75

• • • **i** • • •

Italian. See also pizza
    brown rice pasta, 101, 110, 111,
        116, 118
    Italian Meatballs, 103
    Italian Tomato Sauce, 109
    Lasagna, 116–17
    Lemon Chicken, 124
    Linguine Alfredo-Style, 111
    Spaghetti and Meatballs, 110
    Spaghetti Pie, 112
    Teese mozzarella vegan cheese, 22

• • • **k** • • •

kamut, 27

### l

lactose intolerance. *See also* nondairy dishes
- allergy vs., 38
- nondairy cheese, 22, 38, 118
- signs and symptoms of, 16–17

Lasagna, 116–17
- Barbecue Pulled Pork or Chicken in, 126–27

Lemon Chicken, 124

lentils, 26

Linguine Alfredo-Style, 111

lunch
- All-Day Breakfast Sandwich, 71
- burgers and buns, 24, 49, 102, 103
- Cheddar-Ham Quiche, 68
- Chicken Broth and Chicken Meat, 91
- Chicken Noodle Soup, 92
- Corn and Bacon Chowder, 93
- Corn Bread, 59
- Creamy Tomato Soup, 96
- Crispy Fish or Chicken, 120, 121
- Crispy Oven French Fries, 138, 139
- eating away from home, 29–30, 31
- Egg Salad or Deviled Eggs, 99
- gluten-free, 13
- Grilled Cheese Sandwich, 104, 105
- Ham and Cheese Roll-Ups, 83
- Hummus, 75
- Macaroni and Cheese, 118
- Nachos, 80, 81
- packing, 10
- Pasta Salad, 101
- Pizza, 113–15
- Potato Soup, 94, 95
- Quesadillas and Beyond, 82
- Quiche, 68, 69
- Red Pepper Hummus, 75
- Sarah's Spring Rolls, 84, 85–87
- school, 9
- Spaghetti and Meatballs, 110
- Spaghetti Pie, 112
- Spinach Dip, 76
- Spinach Quiche, 68
- Sweet Potato Fingers with Marshmallow Dip, 79
- Tomato Hummus, 75
- Tuna Salad or Tuna Melt, 100
- Vegetable Quiche, 68
- White Bean Dip, 78

### m

Macaroni and Cheese, 118

main dishes
- Barbecue Baby Back Ribs, 128
- Barbecue Pulled Pork or Chicken, 126–27
- Basic Tomato Sauce, 109
- Cheese Sauce, 119
- Chicken, Broccoli, and Carrot Stir-Fry, 122–23
- Chili Con Carne, 132
- Crispy Fish or Chicken, 120, 121
- Italian Tomato Sauce, 109
- Lasagna, 116–17
- Lemon Chicken, 124
- Linguine Alfredo-Style, 111
- Macaroni and Cheese, 118
- Meat-and-Vegetable Stew du Jour, 129
- Pizza, 113–15
- Shrimp Fried Rice, 133
- Spaghetti and Meatballs, 110
- Spaghetti Pie, 112
- Taco Pie, 130, 131
- Ten-Minute Barbecue Sauce, 125

malt, 27

malt vinegar, 27

Mashed Potatoes or Sweet Potato Mash, 145

meat, 26
- All-Day Breakfast Sandwich, 71
- Barbecue Pulled Pork or Chicken, 126–27
- Basic Burgers or Meatballs, 102, 103
- Beef, Broccoli, and Carrot Stir-Fry, 122–23
- Beef, Chicken, or Turkey Gravy, 140
- Cheddar-Ham Quiche, 68
- Chili Con Carne, 132
- Corn and Bacon Chowder, 93
- as garnish, 94, 104, 144
- Grilled Cheese Sandwich variation, 104, 105
- Ham and Cheese Roll-Ups, 83
- Lasagna, 116–17
- Meat-and-Vegetable Stew du Jour, 129
- Pasta Salad, 101
- Quesadillas and Beyond, 82
- Quiche, 68, 69

medication, as source of gluten, 27

Meringue Surprises, 159

Mexican
- Barbecue Pulled Pork or Chicken tacos, 126–27
- Chili Con Carne, 132
- Green Tomatillo Quesadilla, 82
- Mexican pizza, 78
- Nachos, 80, 81
- Quesadillas and Beyond, 82
- White Bean Dip on quesadillas, 78

mushrooms
- Baked Stuffing, 142, 143
- Meat-and-Vegetable Stew du Jour, 129
- Vegetable Quiche, 68

### n

Nachos, 80, 81

nondairy cheese, 22, 38, 118

nondairy dishes
- All-Day Breakfast Sandwich, 71
- Barbecue Pulled Pork or Chicken, 126–27
- Basic Burgers or Meatballs, 102, 103
- Beef, Chicken, or Turkey Gravy, 140
- burgers and buns, 24, 49, 102, 103
- Chicken, Broccoli, and Carrot Stir-Fry, 122–23
- Chicken Broth and Chicken Meat, 91
- Chicken Noodle Soup, 92
- Chili Con Carne, 132
- Chocolate Glaze, 58
- Cinnamon, Blueberry, or Chocolate Chip Muffins, 66
- Cole Slaw, 137
- Corn and Bacon Chowder, 93
- Crispy Fish or Chicken, 120, 121
- Crispy Oven French Fries, 138, 139
- Dairy-Free Ranch-Style Dressing, 97
- Drop Biscuits, 55
- First Try Apple Buckle Pie, 166–67
- Fluffy Pancakes or Waffles, 52
- French Toast and French Toast Sticks, 54
- Frosting and Filling for Cakes and Cupcakes, 161
- Grilled Cheese Sandwich, 104, 105
- Honey-Mustard Vinaigrette, 98
- Lasagna variation, 116–17

Lemon Chicken, 124
Macaroni and Cheese variation, 118
Meat-and-Vegetable Stew
    du Jour, 129
Pasta Salad, 101
Pork, Broccoli, and Carrot Stir-Fry,
    122–23
Pumpkin Pie variation, 169
Quesadillas and Beyond, 82
Quiche variation, 68
Red French Vinaigrette, 98
Sarah's Spring Rolls, 84, 85–87
Shrimp Fried Rice, 133
Sweet Potato Fingers with
    Marshmallow Dip, 79
Taco Pie variation, 130, 131
Teese mozzarella pizza, 22
Three-Bean and Corn Salad, 147
Tuna Salad, 100
Vanilla Glaze, 58
Vanilla or Chocolate Pudding, 171
nuts, 26, 158

• • • **o** • • •

Oatmeal Cookies, 158
osteoporosis, 15

• • • **p** • • •

packaged foods, 22
pancakes
    Banana Pancakes, 53
    Chocolate Chip Pancakes, 53
    Fluffy Pancakes or Waffles, 52–53
    Strawberry Pancakes, 53
parties. *See also* dessert
    Cakes and Cupcakes Frosting and
        Filling, 161, 162
    Chocolate Cake and Cupcakes, 164
    Chocolate Chip Cookies, 154, 155
    Crispy Oven French Fries, 138, 139
    Deviled Eggs, 99
    Easy-Mix Brownies, 153
    First Try Apple Buckle Pie, 166–67
    Green Onion Dip, 77
    Green Tomatillo Quesadilla, 82
    Ham and Cheese Roll-Ups, 83
    Hummus, 75
    Meringue Surprises, 159
    Nachos, 80, 81
    Oatmeal Cookies, 158
    Pat-in-the-Pan Pie Crust, 168

Pumpkin Pie, 169
Quesadillas and Beyond, 82
Red Pepper Hummus, 75
Sarah's Spring Rolls, 84, 85–87
S'mores and More, 160
Spinach Dip, 76
Strawberry-Blueberry Shortcake
    with Chantilly Cream, 165
Sugar Cookies, 156–57
Sweet Potato Fingers with
    Marshmallow Dip, 79
teen's favorites, 21
Tomato Hummus, 75
Vanilla or Chocolate Pudding,
    170, 171
White Bean Dip, 78
Yellow Cake and Cupcakes, 163
Pasta Salad, 101
Pat-in-the-Pan Pie Crust, 168
peanut butter
    Quesadillas and Beyond, 82
    S'mores and More, 160
pizza
    Barbecue Pulled Pork or Chicken
        topping, 126–27
    Mexican, 78
    as most missed food, 9, 21
    Pizza, 113–15
    as quesadilla variation, 82
    Teese mozzarella vegan, 22
pork
    All-Day Breakfast Sandwich, 71
    bacon as garnish, 94, 104, 144
    Barbecue Pulled Pork or Chicken,
        126–27
    Cheddar-Ham Quiche, 68
    Corn and Bacon Chowder, 93
    Ham and Cheese Roll-Ups, 83
    Meat-and-Vegetable Stew
        du Jour, 129
    Pasta Salad, 101
    Pork, Broccoli, and Carrot Stir-Fry,
        122–23
    Quesadillas and Beyond, 82
    Quiche, 68, 69
potatoes
    Cheesy Scalloped Potatoes, 146
    Mashed Potatoes or Sweet Potato
        Mash, 145
    Meat-and-Vegetable Stew
        du Jour, 129
    Potato Soup, 94, 95
    potato starch flour, 43

Sweet Potato Fingers with
    Marshmallow Dip, 79
poultry, 26. *See also* chicken; turkey
    Meat-and-Vegetable Stew
        du Jour, 129
prepared/packaged foods, 22
pumpkin
    Pumpkin Bread Bars, 62
    Pumpkin Pie, 169

• • • **q** • • •

quesadillas
    Barbecue Pulled Pork or Chicken in,
        126–27
    Quesadillas and Beyond, 82
    White Bean Dip on, 78
quiche, 69
    Cheddar-Ham Quiche, 68
    nondairy, 68
    Spinach Quiche, 68
    Vegetable Quiche, 68
quinoa flour, 43

• • • **r** • • •

Ranch-Style Dressing, 97
Red French Vinaigrette, 98
Red Pepper Hummus, 75
rice
    brown rice pasta, 101, 110, 111,
        116, 118
    Chicken Noodle Soup variation, 92
    flour, 43, 85
    Shrimp Fried Rice, 133
rice milk
    Chocolate Glaze, 58
    Cinnamon, Blueberry, or Chocolate
        Chip Muffins, 66
    Drop Biscuits, 55
    First Try Apple Buckle Pie, 166–67
    Fluffy Pancakes or Waffles, 52
    French Toast and French Toast
        Sticks, 54
    Frosting and Filling for Cakes and
        Cupcakes, 161
    nondairy Pumpkin Pie, 169
    nondairy Quiche, 68
    Vanilla Glaze, 58
    Vanilla or Chocolate Pudding, 171
rye, 27, 50–51

● ● ● **s** ● ● ●

salad dressings
    Dairy-Free Ranch-Style Dressing, 97
    Honey-Mustard Vinaigrette, 98
    Ranch-Style Dressing, 97
    Red French Vinaigrette, 98
salads
    Barbecue Pulled Pork or Chicken in,
       126–27
    Cole Slaw, 137
    Egg Salad or Deviled Eggs, 99
    green, 98
    Pasta Salad, 101
    Three-Bean and Corn Salad, 147
    Tuna Salad or Tuna Melt, 100
sandwiches
    All-Day Breakfast Sandwich, 71
    Barbecue Pulled Pork or Chicken in,
       126–27
    burgers and buns, 24, 49, 102, 103
    Grilled Cheese Sandwich, 104, 105
    Ham and Cheese Roll-Ups, 83
    White Sandwich Bread, 45–47
Sarah's Spring Rolls, 84, 85–87
school lunch, 9
seafood, 26
    Crispy Fish or Chicken, 120, 121
    Quesadillas and Beyond, 82
    Shrimp Fried Rice, 133
semolina, 27
shrimp
    Sarah's Spring Rolls, 84
    Shrimp Fried Rice, 133
side dishes
    Applesauce, 141
    Baked Stuffing, 142, 143
    Beef, Chicken, or Turkey Gravy, 140
    Broccoli, Cauliflower, and
       Cheese, 148
    Cheesy Scalloped Potatoes, 146
    Cole Slaw, 137
    Creamed Spinach, 144
    Crispy Oven French Fries, 138, 139
    green salads, 98
    Mashed Potatoes or Sweet Potato
       Mash, 145
    Three-Bean and Corn Salad, 147
S'mores and More, 160
snacks
    Crispy Fish or Chicken, 120, 121
    gluten-free, 13
    grab and go, 20

    Green Onion Dip, 77
    Ham and Cheese Roll-Ups, 83
    Hummus, 75
    Nachos, 80, 81
    Quesadillas and Beyond, 82
    Red Pepper Hummus, 75
    Sarah's Spring Rolls, 84, 85–87
    Spinach Dip, 76
    Sweet Potato Fingers with
       Marshmallow Dip, 79
    Tomato Hummus, 75
    White Bean Dip, 78
sorghum flour, 43
soups
    Chicken Broth and Chicken
       Meat, 91
    Chicken Noodle Soup, 92
    Corn and Bacon Chowder, 93
    Creamy Tomato Soup, 96
    Meat-and-Vegetable Stew
       du Jour, 129
    Potato Soup, 94, 95
sour cream
    Almond–Sour Cream Coffee
       Cake, 60
    Dairy-Free Ranch-Style Dressing, 97
    Egg Salad or Deviled Eggs, 99
    as garnish, 132
    Green Onion Dip, 77
    Nachos, 80, 81
    Pasta Salad, 101
    Ranch-Style Dressing, 97
    Spinach Dip, 76
    Taco Pie, 130, 131
soy milk
    Chocolate Glaze, 58
    Cinnamon, Blueberry, or Chocolate
       Chip Muffins, 66
    Drop Biscuits, 55
    First Try Apple Buckle Pie, 166–67
    Fluffy Pancakes or Waffles, 52
    French Toast and French Toast
       Sticks, 54
    Frosting and Filling for Cakes and
       Cupcakes, 161
    nondairy Pumpkin Pie, 169
    nondairy Quiche, 68
    Vanilla Glaze, 58
    Vanilla or Chocolate Pudding, 171
soy sauce, 27
Spaghetti and Meatballs, 110
Spaghetti Pie, 112
spelt, 27

spinach
    Creamed Spinach, 144
    Spinach Dip, 76
    Spinach Quiche, 68
starters
    Green Onion Dip, 77
    Ham and Cheese Roll-Ups, 83
    Hummus, 75
    Nachos, 80, 81
    Quesadillas and Beyond, 82
    Red Pepper Hummus, 75
    Sarah's Spring Rolls, 84, 85–87
    Spinach Dip, 76
    Sweet Potato Fingers with
       Marshmallow Dip, 79
    Tomato Hummus, 75
    White Bean Dip, 78
Strawberry Pancakes, 53
Strawberry-Blueberry Shortcake with
    Chantilly Cream, 165
Streusel Topping, 60–61
sweet potatoes
    Sweet Potato Fingers with
       Marshmallow Dip, 79
    Sweet Potato Mash, 145

● ● ● **t** ● ● ●

tacos
    Barbecue Pulled Pork or Chicken in,
       126–27
    Taco Pie, 130, 131
tamari, 27
tapioca starch or flour, 43
Teese mozzarella vegan cheese, 22
teff flour, 26, 50
Ten-Minute Barbecue Sauce, 125
Thanksgiving stuffing, 142
Three-Bean and Corn Salad, 147
thyroid disease, 15
tomatoes
    Barbecue Pulled Pork or Chicken in
       tomato sauce, 126–27
    Basic Tomato Sauce, 109
    Creamy Tomato Soup, 96
    Italian Tomato Sauce, 109
    Tomato Hummus, 75
triticale, 27
Tuna Salad or Tuna Melt, 100
turkey
    Baked Stuffing, 142
    Beef, Chicken, or Turkey Gravy, 140
    Breakfast Sausage Patties, 70

burgers, 24, 49, 102, 103
Chili Con Carne, 132
Ham and Cheese Roll-Ups, 83
Lasagna, 116–17
Meat-and-Vegetable Stew
    du Jour, 129
Quesadillas and Beyond, 82
Spaghetti Pie, 112

• • • u • • •

University of Chicago Celiac Disease
    Center, 27
Unsafe Foods List, 27

• • • v • • •

vanilla
    Vanilla Glaze, 58
    Vanilla or Chocolate Pudding,
        170, 171
    Vanilla Sugar, 63
vegetables, fresh, 6, 26
    Broccoli, Cauliflower, and
        Cheese, 148
    Cheesy Scalloped Potatoes, 146
    Chicken Broth, 91
    Chicken Noodle Soup, 92
    Cole Slaw, 137

Creamed Spinach, 144
Crispy Oven French Fries, 138, 139
Mashed Potatoes or Sweet Potato
    Mash, 145
Meat-and-Vegetable Stew
    du Jour, 129
Sarah's Spring Rolls, 84, 85–87
Spinach Dip, 76
Spinach Quiche, 68
Three-Bean and Corn Salad, 147
Vegetable Quiche, 68
vegetarian
    Applesauce, 141
    Baked Stuffing, 142, 143
    Broccoli, Cauliflower, and Cheese,
        148
    Cheesy Scalloped Potatoes, 146
    Cole Slaw, 137
    Creamed Spinach, 144
    Crispy Oven French Fries, 138, 139
    Green Onion Dip, 77
    Green Tomatillo Quesadilla, 82
    Hummus, 75
    Lasagna, 116–17
    Linguine Alfredo-Style, 111
    Mashed Potatoes or Sweet Potato
        Mash, 145
    Nachos variation, 80, 81
    Pasta Salad, 101

Pizza, 113–15
Quesadillas and Beyond, 82
Red Pepper Hummus, 75
Spinach Dip, 76
Sweet Potato Fingers with
    Marshmallow Dip, 79
Taco Pie variation, 131
Three-Bean and Corn Salad, 147
Tomato Hummus, 75
Vegetable Quiche, 68
Vegetarian Pasta Salad, 101
White Bean Dip, 78

• • • w • • •

waffles, 52–53
wheat, 27
White Bean Dip, 78
white rice flour, 43
White Sandwich Bread, 45–47

• • • x • • •

xanthan gum, 37, 42, 43

• • • y • • •

Yellow Cake and Cupcakes, 163

# about the authors

**Carlyn Berghoff**, CEO of the Berghoff Catering and Restaurant Group, is the fourth generation to continue the Berghoff legacy of serving great food and entertaining guests. She is an author, a chef and restaurateur, a caterer, and a wife and mother. She is a graduate of the Culinary Institute of America and now operates the famous Berghoff restaurants and also catering out of Chicago's century-old Berghoff building. She is the coauthor of *The Berghoff Family Cookbook* and author of *The Berghoff Café Cookbook*. She is married to Jim McClure, and the couple has two daughters and a son. She embraced gluten-free cooking and product and recipe development after her daughter Sarah was diagnosed with celiac disease. (Photo courtesy of Sonia Roselli.)

**Sarah Berghoff McClure** is the second daughter of Jim McClure and Carlyn Berghoff McClure. She attends high school, is the coxswain for a rowing team, and loves to cook. She has two pet lovebirds (she says she's their mother) and a dog named Badger. She liked all the normal teenage foods: fries, cookies, cakes, pizza, stuffing and gravy, and more. In 2009, she became critically ill, lost ten pounds suddenly, and was diagnosed with celiac disease. Since then she has regained her health and vitality and tells everyone she is going to live ten years longer because she is eating gluten free. (Photo courtesy of Sonia Roselli.)

**Suzanne P. Nelson, MD, MPH,** specializes in pediatric gastroenterology and is Assistant Professor of Clinical Pediatrics, The Feinberg School of Medicine, Northwestern University, in Chicago, Illinois. She graduated from Northwestern University Medical School with a Doctor of Medicine (MD) and from Harvard School of Public Health with a Master of Public Health (MPH). She has a busy gastroenterology practice and has been recognized with various awards including U.S. News and World Report's "Top Doctor" status. According to Dr. Nelson, about 1 percent of Americans have celiac disease. Among that 1 percent is Sarah Berghoff McClure, one of Dr. Nelson's patients. And while Dr. Nelson is never happy to tell her patients, "You have celiac disease," she notes. "A part of me is always relieved because I know the child is going to be all right. Celiac disease is one of the few diseases I treat that doesn't require any medication (and therefore no drug side effects) and is 100 percent treatable by diet." Carlyn and Sarah Berghoff McClure are thankful for Dr. Nelson and her role as the adviser and consultant for this cookbook.

**Nancy Ross Ryan** served as the writer for *The Berghoff Family Cookbook* and *The Berghoff Café Cookbook*. She is the founder of Fresh Food Writing in Chicago, Illinois, and specializes in food writing and recipe development.